THIS IS YOUR **PASSBOOK**® FOR ...

HEALTH AIDE

NATIONAL LEARNING CORPORATION®

passbooks.com

PASSBOOK® SERIES

THE *PASSBOOK® SERIES* has been created to prepare applicants and candidates for the ultimate academic battlefield – the examination room.

At some time in our lives, each and every one of us may be required to take an examination – for validation, matriculation, admission, qualification, registration, certification, or licensure.

Based on the assumption that every applicant or candidate has met the basic formal educational standards, has taken the required number of courses, and read the necessary texts, the *PASSBOOK® SERIES* furnishes the one special preparation which may assure passing with confidence, instead of failing with insecurity. Examination questions – together with answers – are furnished as the basic vehicle for study so that the mysteries of the examination and its compounding difficulties may be eliminated or diminished by a sure method.

This book is meant to help you pass your examination provided that you qualify and are serious in your objective.

The entire field is reviewed through the huge store of content information which is succinctly presented through a provocative and challenging approach – the question-and-answer method.

A climate of success is established by furnishing the correct answers at the end of each test.

You soon learn to recognize types of questions, forms of questions, and patterns of questioning. You may even begin to anticipate expected outcomes.

You perceive that many questions are repeated or adapted so that you can gain acute insights, which may enable you to score many sure points.

You learn how to confront new questions, or types of questions, and to attack them confidently and work out the correct answers.

You note objectives and emphases, and recognize pitfalls and dangers, so that you may make positive educational adjustments.

Moreover, you are kept fully informed in relation to new concepts, methods, practices, and directions in the field.

You discover that you arre actually taking the examination all the time: you are preparing for the examination by "taking" an examination, not by reading extraneous and/or supererogatory textbooks.

In short, this PASSBOOK®, used directedly, should be an important factor in helping you to pass your test.

HEALTH AIDE

BASIC FUNCTION:

Under the direction of a school site administrator, screen ill or injured students and administer basic first aid in accordance with State laws and District regulations; assist with health testing/screening programs; prepare and maintain a variety of records, files and reports.

REPRESENTATIVE DUTIES:

Perform basic first aid procedures and screen ill or injured students according to established procedures; utilize a variety of health products and supplies in caring for injuries and health needs.

Administer first aid in emergency situations and notify nurse, administrator, parents or paramedics as necessary.

Schedule students for and assist with the preparation of a variety of examinations pertaining to the health appraisal of students, including physical, vision, and hearing examinations; schedule follow-up appointments if further testing is required; follow up with parent on nurse referrals.

Assist with registration of students regarding health requirements; monitor immunization compliance and follow up with parents as necessary.

Contact parents or other responsible persons regarding ill or injured students; follow up with parents on health issues.

Administer medication to students according to physician instructions and in accordance with State laws and District policies and procedures; monitor renewal of expired medications and orders; perform specialized procedures such as conduct and monitor glucose testing, monitor student self-administration of insulin, administer aerosol nebulizer treatments, and monitor students requiring other health procedures such as tube feedings, tracheotomies, etc.

Prepare, maintain, enter and type a variety of health-related records and files and reports including student health records, emergency medical records, accident and statistical reports; prepare correspondence, forms, notices and referrals; maintain files.

Maintain the health office in a clean, orderly, and safe condition; assist in maintaining inventory and order first aid supplies as necessary; maintain health office equipment. Operate a variety of medical and standard office equipment including a stethoscope and electronic thermometer.

Administer CPR in emergency situations as necessary.

Perform related duties as assigned.

KNOWLEDGE AND ABILITIES:

KNOWLEDGE OF:
CPR and first aid methods and procedures.
District policies and State regulations concerning immunization of school-aged children.
Hygiene and health needs of school-aged children.
Health and medical terminology.
Health and safety regulations.
Applicable sections of State Education Code and other applicable laws.
District organization, operations, policies and objectives.
Modern office practices, procedures and equipment.
Record keeping techniques.
Correct English usage, grammar, spelling punctuation and vocabulary.
Interpersonal skills using tact, patience and courtesy.
Oral and written communication skills.
Telephone techniques and etiquette.

ABILITY TO:
Administer first aid to ill or injured children.
Screen students for various health and safety concerns.
Respond appropriately and effectively to emergency situations.
Establish and maintain files, records, reports and referrals.
Meet schedules and time lines.
Administer medications according to established procedures.
Establish and maintain cooperative and effective working relationships with others.
Plan and organize work.
Work confidentially with discretion.
Communicate effectively both orally and in writing.
Read, interpret, apply and explain laws, rules, regulations, policies and procedures.
Perform clerical duties such as filing, data entry, duplicating typing and maintaining records.
Complete work with many interruptions.
Sit or stand for extended periods of time.
Lift, carry, push or pull students needing assistance.
Bend at the waist, kneel or crouch to assist students.
Reach overhead, above the shoulders and horizontally.
See to assess student illnesses and injuries.

EDUCATION AND EXPERIENCE:
Any combination equivalent to: graduation from high school and six months' experience involving general office work. Experience in a health care service environment is desirable.

LICENSES AND OTHER REQUIREMENTS:
Valid First Aid and CPR Certification issued by an authorized agency. Some positions in this class may require bilingual skills.

WORKING CONDITIONS:
ENVIRONMENT:
Health office environment. Constant interruptions.

HAZARDS:
Contact with blood and other body fluids.
Potential for contact with blood-borne pathogens and communicable diseases.

HOME HEALTH AIDES
PERSONAL AND HOME CARE AIDES

Significant Points
> - Job opportunities are expected to be excellent because of rapid growth in home healthcare and high replacement needs.
> - Training requirements vary from State to State, the type of home services agency, and funding source covering the costs of services.
> - Many of these workers work part time and weekends or evenings to suit the needs of their clients.

Nature of the Work
Home health aides and personal and home care aides help people who are disabled, chronically ill, or cognitively impaired and older adults, who may need assistance, live in their own homes or in residential facilities instead of in health facilities or institutions. They also assist people in hospices and day programs and help individuals with disabilities go to work and remain engaged in their communities. Most aides work with elderly or physically or mentally disabled clients who need more care than family or friends can provide. Others help discharge hospital patients who have relatively short-term needs.

Aides provide light housekeeping and homemaking tasks such as laundry, change bed linens, shop for food, plan and prepare meals. Aides also may help clients get out of bed, bathe, dress, and groom. Some accompany clients to doctors' appointments or on other errands.

Home health aides and personal and home care aides provide instruction and psychological support to their clients. They may advise families and patients on nutrition, cleanliness, and household tasks.

Aides' daily routine may vary. They may go to the same home every day or week for months or even years and often visit four or five clients on the same day. However, some aides may work solely with one client who is in need of more care and attention. In some situations, this may involve working with other aides in shifts so that the client has an aide throughout the day and night. Aides also work with clients, particularly younger adults at schools or at the client's work site.

In general, home health aides and personal and home care aides have similar job duties. However, there are some small differences.

Home health aides typically work for certified home health or hospice agencies that receive government funding and therefore must comply with regulations from to receive funding. This means that they must work under the direct supervision of a medical professional, usually a nurse. These aides keep records of services performed and of clients' condition and progress. They report changes in the client's condition to the supervisor or case manager. Aides also work with therapists and other medical staff.

Home health aides may provide some basic health-related services, such as checking patients' pulse rate, temperature, and respiration rate. They also may help with simple prescribed exercises and assist with medications administration. Occasionally, they change simple dressings, give massages, provide skin care, or assist with braces and artificial limbs.

With special training, experienced home health aides also may assist with medical equipment such as ventilators, which help patients breathe.

Personal and home care aides-also called homemakers, caregivers, companions, and personal attendants-work for various public and private agencies that provide home care services. In these agencies, caregivers are likely supervised by a licensed nurse, social worker, or other non-medical managers. Aides receive detailed instructions explaining when to visit clients and what services to perform for them.

However, personal and home care aides work independently, with only periodic visits by their supervisor These caregivers may work with only one client each day or five or six clients once a day every week or every 2 weeks.

Some aides are hired directly by the patient or the patient's family. In these situations, personal and home care aides are supervised and assigned tasks directly by the patient or the patient's family.

Aides may also work with individuals who are developmentally or intellectually disabled. These workers are often called direct support professionals and they may assist in implementing a behavior plan, teaching self-care skills and providing employment support, as well as providing a range of other personal assistance services

Work environment

Work as an aide can be physically demanding. Aides must guard against back injury because they may have to move patients into and out of bed or help them to stand or walk. Aides also may face hazards from minor infections and exposure to communicable diseases, such as hepatitis, but can avoid infections by following proper procedures. Because mechanical lifting devices available in institutional settings are not as frequently available in patients' homes, home health aides must take extra care to avoid injuries resulting from overexertion when they assist patients. These workers experienced a larger than average number of work-related injuries or illnesses.

Aides also perform tasks that some may consider unpleasant, such as emptying bedpans and changing soiled bed linens. The patients they care for may be disoriented, irritable, or uncooperative. Although their work can be emotionally demanding, many aides gain satisfaction from assisting those in need

Most aides work with a number of different patients, each job lasting a few hours, days, or weeks. They often visit multiple patients on the same day. Surroundings differ by case. Some homes are neat and pleasant, whereas others are untidy and depressing. Some clients are pleasant and cooperative; others are angry, abusive, depressed, or otherwise difficult.

Home health aides and personal and home care aides generally work alone, with periodic visits from their supervisor. They receive detailed instructions explaining when to visit patients and what services to perform. Aides are responsible for getting to patients' homes, and they may spend a good portion of the work day traveling from one patient to another.

Many of these workers work part time and weekends or evenings to suit the needs of their clients.

Training, Other Qualifications, and Advancement

Home health aides must receive formal training and pass a competency test to work for certified home health or hospice agencies that receive reimbursement from Medicare or Medicaid. Personal and home care aides, however, face a wide range of requirements, which vary from State to State.

Education and training. Home health aides and personal and home care aides are generally not required to have a high school diploma. They usually are trained on the job by registered nurses, licensed practical nurses, experienced aides, or their supervisor. Aides are instructed on how to cook for a client, including on special diets. Furthermore, they may be trained in basic housekeeping tasks, such as making a bed and keeping the home sanitary and safe for the client. Generally, they are taught how to respond to an emergency, learning basic safety techniques. Employers also may train aides to conduct themselves in a professional and courteous manner while in a client's home. Some clients prefer that tasks are done a certain way and will teach the aide. A competency evaluation may be required to ensure that the aide can perform the required tasks.

Licensure
Home health aides who work for agencies that receive reimbursement from Medicare or Medicaid must receive a minimum level of training. They must complete both a training program consisting of a minimum of 75 hours and a competency evaluation or state certification program. Training includes information regarding personal hygiene, safe transfer techniques, reading and recording vital signs, infection control, and basic nutrition. Aides may take a competency exam to become certified without taking any of the training. At a minimum, 16 hours of supervised practical training are required before an aide has direct contact with a resident. These certification requirements represent the minimum, as outlined by the Federal Government. Some States may require additional hours of training to become certified.

Personal and home care aides are not required to be certified.

Other qualifications. Aides should have a desire to help people. They should be responsible, compassionate, patient, emotionally stable, and cheerful. In addition, aides should be tactful, honest, and discreet, because they work in private homes. Aides also must be in good health.
A physical examination, including State-mandated tests for tuberculosis and other diseases, may be required. A criminal background check and a good driving record also may be required for employment.

Certification and advancement. The National Association for Home Care and Hospice (NAHC) offers national certification for aides. Certification is a voluntary demonstration that the individual has met industry standards. Certification requires the completion of 75 hours of training; observation and documentation of 17 skills for competency, assessed by a registered nurse; and the passing of a written exam developed by NAHC.

Advancement for home health aides and personal and home care aides is limited. In some agencies, workers start out performing homemaker duties, such as cleaning. With experience and training, they may take on more personal care duties. Some aides choose to receive additional training to become nursing aides, licensed practical nurses, or registered nurses. Some may start their own home care agency or work as a self-employed aide. Self-employed aides have no agency affiliation or supervision and accept clients, set fees, and arrange work schedules on their own.

Employment
Home health aides and personal and home care aides hold about 1.7 million jobs. The majority of jobs were in home healthcare services, individual and family services, residential care facilities, and private households.

Job Outlook
Excellent job opportunities are expected for this occupation because rapid employment growth and high replacement needs are projected to produce a large number of job openings.

Employment change. Employment of home health aides is projected to grow by 50 percent by 2020, which is much faster than the average for all occupations. Employment of personal and home care aides is also expected to grow by 50 percent by 2020, which is much faster than the average for all occupations. For both occupations, the expected growth is due, in large part, to the projected rise in the number of elderly people, an age group that often has mounting health problems and that needs some assistance with daily activities. The elderly and other clients, such as the mentally disabled, increasingly rely on home care.

This trend reflects several developments. Inpatient care in hospitals and nursing homes can be extremely expensive, so more patients return to their homes from these facilities as quickly as possible in order to contain costs. Patients, who need assistance with everyday tasks and household chores rather than medical care, can reduce medical expenses by returning to their homes. Furthermore, most patients--particularly the elderly--prefer care in their homes rather than in nursing homes or other in-patient facilities. This development is aided by the realization that treatment can be more effective in familiar surroundings.

Job prospects. In addition to job openings created by the increased demand for these workers, replacement needs are expected to lead to many openings. The relatively low skill requirements, low pay, and high emotional demands of the work result in high replacement needs. For these same reasons, many people are reluctant to seek jobs in the occupation. Therefore, persons who are interested in and suited for this work--particularly those with experience or training as personal care, home health, or nursing aides--should have excellent job prospects.

———

HOW TO TAKE A TEST

I. YOU MUST PASS AN EXAMINATION

A. WHAT EVERY CANDIDATE SHOULD KNOW

Examination applicants often ask us for help in preparing for the written test. What can I study in advance? What kinds of questions will be asked? How will the test be given? How will the papers be graded?

As an applicant for a civil service examination, you may be wondering about some of these things. Our purpose here is to suggest effective methods of advance study and to describe civil service examinations.

Your chances for success on this examination can be increased if you know how to prepare. Those "pre-examination jitters" can be reduced if you know what to expect. You can even experience an adventure in good citizenship if you know why civil service exams are given.

B. WHY ARE CIVIL SERVICE EXAMINATIONS GIVEN?

Civil service examinations are important to you in two ways. As a citizen, you want public jobs filled by employees who know how to do their work. As a job seeker, you want a fair chance to compete for that job on an equal footing with other candidates. The best-known means of accomplishing this two-fold goal is the competitive examination.

Exams are widely publicized throughout the nation. They may be administered for jobs in federal, state, city, municipal, town or village governments or agencies.

Any citizen may apply, with some limitations, such as the age or residence of applicants. Your experience and education may be reviewed to see whether you meet the requirements for the particular examination. When these requirements exist, they are reasonable and applied consistently to all applicants. Thus, a competitive examination may cause you some uneasiness now, but it is your privilege and safeguard.

C. HOW ARE CIVIL SERVICE EXAMS DEVELOPED?

Examinations are carefully written by trained technicians who are specialists in the field known as "psychological measurement," in consultation with recognized authorities in the field of work that the test will cover. These experts recommend the subject matter areas or skills to be tested; only those knowledges or skills important to your success on the job are included. The most reliable books and source materials available are used as references. Together, the experts and technicians judge the difficulty level of the questions.

Test technicians know how to phrase questions so that the problem is clearly stated. Their ethics do not permit "trick" or "catch" questions. Questions may have been tried out on sample groups, or subjected to statistical analysis, to determine their usefulness.

Written tests are often used in combination with performance tests, ratings of training and experience, and oral interviews. All of these measures combine to form the best-known means of finding the right person for the right job.

II. HOW TO PASS THE WRITTEN TEST

A. NATURE OF THE EXAMINATION

To prepare intelligently for civil service examinations, you should know how they differ from school examinations you have taken. In school you were assigned certain definite pages to read or subjects to cover. The examination questions were quite detailed and usually emphasized memory. Civil service exams, on the other hand, try to discover your present ability to perform the duties of a position, plus your potentiality to learn these duties. In other words, a civil service exam attempts to predict how successful you will be. Questions cover such a broad area that they cannot be as minute and detailed as school exam questions.

In the public service similar kinds of work, or positions, are grouped together in one "class." This process is known as *position-classification*. All the positions in a class are paid according to the salary range for that class. One class title covers all of these positions, and they are all tested by the same examination.

B. FOUR BASIC STEPS

1) Study the announcement

How, then, can you know what subjects to study? Our best answer is: "Learn as much as possible about the class of positions for which you've applied." The exam will test the knowledge, skills and abilities needed to do the work.

Your most valuable source of information about the position you want is the official exam announcement. This announcement lists the training and experience qualifications. Check these standards and apply only if you come reasonably close to meeting them.

The brief description of the position in the examination announcement offers some clues to the subjects which will be tested. Think about the job itself. Review the duties in your mind. Can you perform them, or are there some in which you are rusty? Fill in the blank spots in your preparation.

Many jurisdictions preview the written test in the exam announcement by including a section called "Knowledge and Abilities Required," "Scope of the Examination," or some similar heading. Here you will find out specifically what fields will be tested.

2) Review your own background

Once you learn in general what the position is all about, and what you need to know to do the work, ask yourself which subjects you already know fairly well and which need improvement. You may wonder whether to concentrate on improving your strong areas or on building some background in your fields of weakness. When the announcement has specified "some knowledge" or "considerable knowledge," or has used adjectives like "beginning principles of..." or "advanced ... methods," you can get a clue as to the number and difficulty of questions to be asked in any given field. More questions, and hence broader coverage, would be included for those subjects which are more important in the work. Now weigh your strengths and weaknesses against the job requirements and prepare accordingly.

3) Determine the level of the position
Another way to tell how intensively you should prepare is to understand the level of the job for which you are applying. Is it the entering level? In other words, is this the position in which beginners in a field of work are hired? Or is it an intermediate or advanced level? Sometimes this is indicated by such words as "Junior" or "Senior" in the class title. Other jurisdictions use Roman numerals to designate the level – Clerk I, Clerk II, for example. The word "Supervisor" sometimes appears in the title. If the level is not indicated by the title, check the description of duties. Will you be working under very close supervision, or will you have responsibility for independent decisions in this work?

4) Choose appropriate study materials
Now that you know the subjects to be examined and the relative amount of each subject to be covered, you can choose suitable study materials. For beginning level jobs, or even advanced ones, if you have a pronounced weakness in some aspect of your training, read a modern, standard textbook in that field. Be sure it is up to date and has general coverage. Such books are normally available at your library, and the librarian will be glad to help you locate one. For entry-level positions, questions of appropriate difficulty are chosen – neither highly advanced questions, nor those too simple. Such questions require careful thought but not advanced training.

If the position for which you are applying is technical or advanced, you will read more advanced, specialized material. If you are already familiar with the basic principles of your field, elementary textbooks would waste your time. Concentrate on advanced textbooks and technical periodicals. Think through the concepts and review difficult problems in your field.

These are all general sources. You can get more ideas on your own initiative, following these leads. For example, training manuals and publications of the government agency which employs workers in your field can be useful, particularly for technical and professional positions. A letter or visit to the government department involved may result in more specific study suggestions, and certainly will provide you with a more definite idea of the exact nature of the position you are seeking.

III. KINDS OF TESTS

Tests are used for purposes other than measuring knowledge and ability to perform specified duties. For some positions, it is equally important to test ability to make adjustments to new situations or to profit from training. In others, basic mental abilities not dependent on information are essential. Questions which test these things may not appear as pertinent to the duties of the position as those which test for knowledge and information. Yet they are often highly important parts of a fair examination. For very general questions, it is almost impossible to help you direct your study efforts. What we can do is to point out some of the more common of these general abilities needed in public service positions and describe some typical questions.

1) General information
Broad, general information has been found useful for predicting job success in some kinds of work. This is tested in a variety of ways, from vocabulary lists to questions about current events. Basic background in some field of work, such as

sociology or economics, may be sampled in a group of questions. Often these are principles which have become familiar to most persons through exposure rather than through formal training. It is difficult to advise you how to study for these questions; being alert to the world around you is our best suggestion.

2) Verbal ability

An example of an ability needed in many positions is verbal or language ability. Verbal ability is, in brief, the ability to use and understand words. Vocabulary and grammar tests are typical measures of this ability. Reading comprehension or paragraph interpretation questions are common in many kinds of civil service tests. You are given a paragraph of written material and asked to find its central meaning.

3) Numerical ability

Number skills can be tested by the familiar arithmetic problem, by checking paired lists of numbers to see which are alike and which are different, or by interpreting charts and graphs. In the latter test, a graph may be printed in the test booklet which you are asked to use as the basis for answering questions.

4) Observation

A popular test for law-enforcement positions is the observation test. A picture is shown to you for several minutes, then taken away. Questions about the picture test your ability to observe both details and larger elements.

5) Following directions

In many positions in the public service, the employee must be able to carry out written instructions dependably and accurately. You may be given a chart with several columns, each column listing a variety of information. The questions require you to carry out directions involving the information given in the chart.

6) Skills and aptitudes

Performance tests effectively measure some manual skills and aptitudes. When the skill is one in which you are trained, such as typing or shorthand, you can practice. These tests are often very much like those given in business school or high school courses. For many of the other skills and aptitudes, however, no short-time preparation can be made. Skills and abilities natural to you or that you have developed throughout your lifetime are being tested.

Many of the general questions just described provide all the data needed to answer the questions and ask you to use your reasoning ability to find the answers. Your best preparation for these tests, as well as for tests of facts and ideas, is to be at your physical and mental best. You, no doubt, have your own methods of getting into an exam-taking mood and keeping "in shape." The next section lists some ideas on this subject.

IV. KINDS OF QUESTIONS

Only rarely is the "essay" question, which you answer in narrative form, used in civil service tests. Civil service tests are usually of the short-answer type. Full instructions for answering these questions will be given to you at the examination. But in case this is your first experience with short-answer questions and separate answer sheets, here is what you need to know:

1) Multiple-choice Questions

Most popular of the short-answer questions is the "multiple choice" or "best answer" question. It can be used, for example, to test for factual knowledge, ability to solve problems or judgment in meeting situations found at work.

A multiple-choice question is normally one of three types—

- It can begin with an incomplete statement followed by several possible endings. You are to find the one ending which *best* completes the statement, although some of the others may not be entirely wrong.
- It can also be a complete statement in the form of a question which is answered by choosing one of the statements listed.
- It can be in the form of a problem – again you select the best answer.

Here is an example of a multiple-choice question with a discussion which should give you some clues as to the method for choosing the right answer:

When an employee has a complaint about his assignment, the action which will *best* help him overcome his difficulty is to
- A. discuss his difficulty with his coworkers
- B. take the problem to the head of the organization
- C. take the problem to the person who gave him the assignment
- D. say nothing to anyone about his complaint

In answering this question, you should study each of the choices to find which is best. Consider choice "A" – Certainly an employee may discuss his complaint with fellow employees, but no change or improvement can result, and the complaint remains unresolved. Choice "B" is a poor choice since the head of the organization probably does not know what assignment you have been given, and taking your problem to him is known as "going over the head" of the supervisor. The supervisor, or person who made the assignment, is the person who can clarify it or correct any injustice. Choice "C" is, therefore, correct. To say nothing, as in choice "D," is unwise. Supervisors have and interest in knowing the problems employees are facing, and the employee is seeking a solution to his problem.

2) True/False Questions

The "true/false" or "right/wrong" form of question is sometimes used. Here a complete statement is given. Your job is to decide whether the statement is right or wrong.

SAMPLE: A roaming cell-phone call to a nearby city costs less than a non-roaming call to a distant city.

This statement is wrong, or false, since roaming calls are more expensive.

This is not a complete list of all possible question forms, although most of the others are variations of these common types. You will always get complete directions for answering questions. Be sure you understand *how* to mark your answers – ask questions until you do.

V. RECORDING YOUR ANSWERS

Computer terminals are used more and more today for many different kinds of exams.

For an examination with very few applicants, you may be told to record your answers in the test booklet itself. Separate answer sheets are much more common. If this separate answer sheet is to be scored by machine – and this is often the case – it is highly important that you mark your answers correctly in order to get credit.

An electronic scoring machine is often used in civil service offices because of the speed with which papers can be scored. Machine-scored answer sheets must be marked with a pencil, which will be given to you. This pencil has a high graphite content which responds to the electronic scoring machine. As a matter of fact, stray dots may register as answers, so do not let your pencil rest on the answer sheet while you are pondering the correct answer. Also, if your pencil lead breaks or is otherwise defective, ask for another.

Since the answer sheet will be dropped in a slot in the scoring machine, be careful not to bend the corners or get the paper crumpled.

The answer sheet normally has five vertical columns of numbers, with 30 numbers to a column. These numbers correspond to the question numbers in your test booklet. After each number, going across the page are four or five pairs of dotted lines. These short dotted lines have small letters or numbers above them. The first two pairs may also have a "T" or "F" above the letters. This indicates that the first two pairs only are to be used if the questions are of the true-false type. If the questions are multiple choice, disregard the "T" and "F" and pay attention only to the small letters or numbers.

Answer your questions in the manner of the sample that follows:

32. The largest city in the United States is
      A. Washington, D.C.
      B. New York City
      C. Chicago
      D. Detroit
      E. San Francisco

1) Choose the answer you think is best. (New York City is the largest, so "B" is correct.)
2) Find the row of dotted lines numbered the same as the question you are answering. (Find row number 32)
3) Find the pair of dotted lines corresponding to the answer. (Find the pair of lines under the mark "B.")
4) Make a solid black mark between the dotted lines.

VI. BEFORE THE TEST

Common sense will help you find procedures to follow to get ready for an examination. Too many of us, however, overlook these sensible measures. Indeed, nervousness and fatigue have been found to be the most serious reasons why applicants fail to do their best on civil service tests. Here is a list of reminders:

- Begin your preparation early – Don't wait until the last minute to go scurrying around for books and materials or to find out what the position is all about.
- Prepare continuously – An hour a night for a week is better than an all-night cram session. This has been definitely established. What is more, a night a week for a month will return better dividends than crowding your study into a shorter period of time.
- Locate the place of the exam – You have been sent a notice telling you when and where to report for the examination. If the location is in a different town or otherwise unfamiliar to you, it would be well to inquire the best route and learn something about the building.
- Relax the night before the test – Allow your mind to rest. Do not study at all that night. Plan some mild recreation or diversion; then go to bed early and get a good night's sleep.
- Get up early enough to make a leisurely trip to the place for the test – This way unforeseen events, traffic snarls, unfamiliar buildings, etc. will not upset you.
- Dress comfortably – A written test is not a fashion show. You will be known by number and not by name, so wear something comfortable.
- Leave excess paraphernalia at home – Shopping bags and odd bundles will get in your way. You need bring only the items mentioned in the official notice you received; usually everything you need is provided. Do not bring reference books to the exam. They will only confuse those last minutes and be taken away from you when in the test room.
- Arrive somewhat ahead of time – If because of transportation schedules you must get there very early, bring a newspaper or magazine to take your mind off yourself while waiting.
- Locate the examination room – When you have found the proper room, you will be directed to the seat or part of the room where you will sit. Sometimes you are given a sheet of instructions to read while you are waiting. Do not fill out any forms until you are told to do so; just read them and be prepared.
- Relax and prepare to listen to the instructions
- If you have any physical problem that may keep you from doing your best, be sure to tell the test administrator. If you are sick or in poor health, you really cannot do your best on the exam. You can come back and take the test some other time.

VII. AT THE TEST

The day of the test is here and you have the test booklet in your hand. The temptation to get going is very strong. Caution! There is more to success than knowing the right answers. You must know how to identify your papers and understand variations in the type of short-answer question used in this particular examination. Follow these suggestions for maximum results from your efforts:

1) Cooperate with the monitor

The test administrator has a duty to create a situation in which you can be as much at ease as possible. He will give instructions, tell you when to begin, check to see that you are marking your answer sheet correctly, and so on. He is not there to guard you, although he will see that your competitors do not take unfair advantage. He wants to help you do your best.

2) Listen to all instructions

Don't jump the gun! Wait until you understand all directions. In most civil service tests you get more time than you need to answer the questions. So don't be in a hurry. Read each word of instructions until you clearly understand the meaning. Study the examples, listen to all announcements and follow directions. Ask questions if you do not understand what to do.

3) Identify your papers

Civil service exams are usually identified by number only. You will be assigned a number; you must not put your name on your test papers. Be sure to copy your number correctly. Since more than one exam may be given, copy your exact examination title.

4) Plan your time

Unless you are told that a test is a "speed" or "rate of work" test, speed itself is usually not important. Time enough to answer all the questions will be provided, but this does not mean that you have all day. An overall time limit has been set. Divide the total time (in minutes) by the number of questions to determine the approximate time you have for each question.

5) Do not linger over difficult questions

If you come across a difficult question, mark it with a paper clip (useful to have along) and come back to it when you have been through the booklet. One caution if you do this – be sure to skip a number on your answer sheet as well. Check often to be sure that you have not lost your place and that you are marking in the row numbered the same as the question you are answering.

6) Read the questions

Be sure you know what the question asks! Many capable people are unsuccessful because they failed to *read* the questions correctly.

7) Answer all questions

Unless you have been instructed that a penalty will be deducted for incorrect answers, it is better to guess than to omit a question.

8) Speed tests

It is often better NOT to guess on speed tests. It has been found that on timed tests people are tempted to spend the last few seconds before time is called in marking answers at random – without even reading them – in the hope of picking up a few extra points. To discourage this practice, the instructions may warn you that your score will be "corrected" for guessing. That is, a penalty will be applied. The incorrect answers will be deducted from the correct ones, or some other penalty formula will be used.

9) Review your answers

If you finish before time is called, go back to the questions you guessed or omitted to give them further thought. Review other answers if you have time.

10) Return your test materials

If you are ready to leave before others have finished or time is called, take ALL your materials to the monitor and leave quietly. Never take any test material with you. The monitor can discover whose papers are not complete, and taking a test booklet may be grounds for disqualification.

VIII. EXAMINATION TECHNIQUES

1) Read the general instructions carefully. These are usually printed on the first page of the exam booklet. As a rule, these instructions refer to the timing of the examination; the fact that you should not start work until the signal and must stop work at a signal, etc. If there are any *special* instructions, such as a choice of questions to be answered, make sure that you note this instruction carefully.

2) When you are ready to start work on the examination, that is as soon as the signal has been given, read the instructions to each question booklet, underline any key words or phrases, such as *least, best, outline, describe* and the like. In this way you will tend to answer as requested rather than discover on reviewing your paper that you *listed without describing*, that you selected the *worst* choice rather than the *best* choice, etc.

3) If the examination is of the objective or multiple-choice type – that is, each question will also give a series of possible answers: A, B, C or D, and you are called upon to select the best answer and write the letter next to that answer on your answer paper – it is advisable to start answering each question in turn. There may be anywhere from 50 to 100 such questions in the three or four hours allotted and you can see how much time would be taken if you read through all the questions before beginning to answer any. Furthermore, if you come across a question or group of questions which you know would be difficult to answer, it would undoubtedly affect your handling of all the other questions.

4) If the examination is of the essay type and contains but a few questions, it is a moot point as to whether you should read all the questions before starting to answer any one. Of course, if you are given a choice – say five out of seven and the like – then it is essential to read all the questions so you can eliminate the two that are most difficult. If, however, you are asked to answer all the questions, there may be danger in trying to answer the easiest one first because you may find that you will spend too much time on it. The best technique is to answer the first question, then proceed to the second, etc.

5) Time your answers. Before the exam begins, write down the time it started, then add the time allowed for the examination and write down the time it must be completed, then divide the time available somewhat as follows:

- If 3-1/2 hours are allowed, that would be 210 minutes. If you have 80 objective-type questions, that would be an average of 2-1/2 minutes per question. Allow yourself no more than 2 minutes per question, or a total of 160 minutes, which will permit about 50 minutes to review.
- If for the time allotment of 210 minutes there are 7 essay questions to answer, that would average about 30 minutes a question. Give yourself only 25 minutes per question so that you have about 35 minutes to review.

6) The most important instruction is to *read each question* and make sure you know what is wanted. The second most important instruction is to *time yourself properly* so that you answer every question. The third most important instruction is to *answer every question*. Guess if you have to but include something for each question. Remember that you will receive no credit for a blank and will probably receive some credit if you write something in answer to an essay question. If you guess a letter – say "B" for a multiple-choice question – you may have guessed right. If you leave a blank as an answer to a multiple-choice question, the examiners may respect your feelings but it will not add a point to your score. Some exams may penalize you for wrong answers, so in such cases *only*, you may not want to guess unless you have some basis for your answer.

7) Suggestions
   a. Objective-type questions
      1. Examine the question booklet for proper sequence of pages and questions
      2. Read all instructions carefully
      3. Skip any question which seems too difficult; return to it after all other questions have been answered
      4. Apportion your time properly; do not spend too much time on any single question or group of questions
      5. Note and underline key words – *all, most, fewest, least, best, worst, same, opposite,* etc.
      6. Pay particular attention to negatives
      7. Note unusual option, e.g., unduly long, short, complex, different or similar in content to the body of the question
      8. Observe the use of "hedging" words – *probably, may, most likely,* etc.
      9. Make sure that your answer is put next to the same number as the question
      10. Do not second-guess unless you have good reason to believe the second answer is definitely more correct
      11. Cross out original answer if you decide another answer is more accurate; do not erase until you are ready to hand your paper in
      12. Answer all questions; guess unless instructed otherwise
      13. Leave time for review

   b. Essay questions
      1. Read each question carefully
      2. Determine exactly what is wanted. Underline key words or phrases.
      3. Decide on outline or paragraph answer

4. Include many different points and elements unless asked to develop any one or two points or elements
5. Show impartiality by giving pros and cons unless directed to select one side only
6. Make and write down any assumptions you find necessary to answer the questions
7. Watch your English, grammar, punctuation and choice of words
8. Time your answers; don't crowd material

8) Answering the essay question

Most essay questions can be answered by framing the specific response around several key words or ideas. Here are a few such key words or ideas:

M's: manpower, materials, methods, money, management
P's: purpose, program, policy, plan, procedure, practice, problems, pitfalls, personnel, public relations
   a. Six basic steps in handling problems:
     1. Preliminary plan and background development
     2. Collect information, data and facts
     3. Analyze and interpret information, data and facts
     4. Analyze and develop solutions as well as make recommendations
     5. Prepare report and sell recommendations
     6. Install recommendations and follow up effectiveness

   b. Pitfalls to avoid
     1. *Taking things for granted* – A statement of the situation does not necessarily imply that each of the elements is necessarily true; for example, a complaint may be invalid and biased so that all that can be taken for granted is that a complaint has been registered
     2. *Considering only one side of a situation* – Wherever possible, indicate several alternatives and then point out the reasons you selected the best one
     3. *Failing to indicate follow up* – Whenever your answer indicates action on your part, make certain that you will take proper follow-up action to see how successful your recommendations, procedures or actions turn out to be
     4. *Taking too long in answering any single question* – Remember to time your answers properly

IX. AFTER THE TEST

Scoring procedures differ in detail among civil service jurisdictions although the general principles are the same. Whether the papers are hand-scored or graded by machine we have described, they are nearly always graded by number. That is, the person who marks the paper knows only the number – never the name – of the applicant. Not until all the papers have been graded will they be matched with names. If other tests, such as training and experience or oral interview ratings have been given, scores will be combined. Different parts of the examination usually have different weights. For example, the written test might count 60 percent of the final grade, and a rating of training and experience 40 percent. In many jurisdictions, veterans will have a certain number of points added to their grades.

After the final grade has been determined, the names are placed in grade order and an eligible list is established. There are various methods for resolving ties between those who get the same final grade – probably the most common is to place first the name of the person whose application was received first. Job offers are made from the eligible list in the order the names appear on it. You will be notified of your grade and your rank as soon as all these computations have been made. This will be done as rapidly as possible.

People who are found to meet the requirements in the announcement are called "eligibles." Their names are put on a list of eligible candidates. An eligible's chances of getting a job depend on how high he stands on this list and how fast agencies are filling jobs from the list.

When a job is to be filled from a list of eligibles, the agency asks for the names of people on the list of eligibles for that job. When the civil service commission receives this request, it sends to the agency the names of the three people highest on this list. Or, if the job to be filled has specialized requirements, the office sends the agency the names of the top three persons who meet these requirements from the general list.

The appointing officer makes a choice from among the three people whose names were sent to him. If the selected person accepts the appointment, the names of the others are put back on the list to be considered for future openings.

That is the rule in hiring from all kinds of eligible lists, whether they are for typist, carpenter, chemist, or something else. For every vacancy, the appointing officer has his choice of any one of the top three eligibles on the list. This explains why the person whose name is on top of the list sometimes does not get an appointment when some of the persons lower on the list do. If the appointing officer chooses the second or third eligible, the No. 1 eligible does not get a job at once, but stays on the list until he is appointed or the list is terminated.

X. HOW TO PASS THE INTERVIEW TEST

The examination for which you applied requires an oral interview test. You have already taken the written test and you are now being called for the interview test – the final part of the formal examination.

You may think that it is not possible to prepare for an interview test and that there are no procedures to follow during an interview. Our purpose is to point out some things you can do in advance that will help you and some good rules to follow and pitfalls to avoid while you are being interviewed.

What is an interview supposed to test?

The written examination is designed to test the technical knowledge and competence of the candidate; the oral is designed to evaluate intangible qualities, not readily measured otherwise, and to establish a list showing the relative fitness of each candidate – as measured against his competitors – for the position sought. Scoring is not on the basis of "right" and "wrong," but on a sliding scale of values ranging from "not passable" to "outstanding." As a matter of fact, it is possible to achieve a relatively low score without a single "incorrect" answer because of evident weakness in the qualities being measured.

Occasionally, an examination may consist entirely of an oral test – either an individual or a group oral. In such cases, information is sought concerning the technical knowledges and abilities of the candidate, since there has been no written examination for this purpose. More commonly, however, an oral test is used to supplement a written examination.

Who conducts interviews?

The composition of oral boards varies among different jurisdictions. In nearly all, a representative of the personnel department serves as chairman. One of the members of the board may be a representative of the department in which the candidate would work. In some cases, "outside experts" are used, and, frequently, a businessman or some other representative of the general public is asked to serve. Labor and management or other special groups may be represented. The aim is to secure the services of experts in the appropriate field.

However the board is composed, it is a good idea (and not at all improper or unethical) to ascertain in advance of the interview who the members are and what groups they represent. When you are introduced to them, you will have some idea of their backgrounds and interests, and at least you will not stutter and stammer over their names.

What should be done before the interview?

While knowledge about the board members is useful and takes some of the surprise element out of the interview, there is other preparation which is more substantive. It *is* possible to prepare for an oral interview – in several ways:

1) Keep a copy of your application and review it carefully before the interview

This may be the only document before the oral board, and the starting point of the interview. Know what education and experience you have listed there, and the sequence and dates of all of it. Sometimes the board will ask you to review the highlights of your experience for them; you should not have to hem and haw doing it.

2) Study the class specification and the examination announcement

Usually, the oral board has one or both of these to guide them. The qualities, characteristics or knowledges required by the position sought are stated in these documents. They offer valuable clues as to the nature of the oral interview. For example, if the job involves supervisory responsibilities, the announcement will usually indicate that knowledge of modern supervisory methods and the qualifications of the candidate as a supervisor will be tested. If so, you can expect such questions, frequently in the form of a hypothetical situation which you are expected to solve. NEVER go into an oral without knowledge of the duties and responsibilities of the job you seek.

3) Think through each qualification required

Try to visualize the kind of questions you would ask if you were a board member. How well could you answer them? Try especially to appraise your own knowledge and background in each area, *measured against the job sought*, and identify any areas in which you are weak. Be critical and realistic – do not flatter yourself.

4) Do some general reading in areas in which you feel you may be weak

For example, if the job involves supervision and your past experience has NOT, some general reading in supervisory methods and practices, particularly in the field of human relations, might be useful. Do NOT study agency procedures or detailed manuals. The oral board will be testing your understanding and capacity, not your memory.

5) Get a good night's sleep and watch your general health and mental attitude

You will want a clear head at the interview. Take care of a cold or any other minor ailment, and of course, no hangovers.

What should be done on the day of the interview?

Now comes the day of the interview itself. Give yourself plenty of time to get there. Plan to arrive somewhat ahead of the scheduled time, particularly if your appointment is in the fore part of the day. If a previous candidate fails to appear, the board might be ready for you a bit early. By early afternoon an oral board is almost invariably behind schedule if there are many candidates, and you may have to wait. Take along a book or magazine to read, or your application to review, but leave any extraneous material in the waiting room when you go in for your interview. In any event, relax and compose yourself.

The matter of dress is important. The board is forming impressions about you – from your experience, your manners, your attitude, and your appearance. Give your personal appearance careful attention. Dress your best, but not your flashiest. Choose conservative, appropriate clothing, and be sure it is immaculate. This is a business interview, and your appearance should indicate that you regard it as such. Besides, being well groomed and properly dressed will help boost your confidence.

Sooner or later, someone will call your name and escort you into the interview room. *This is it.* From here on you are on your own. It is too late for any more preparation. But remember, you asked for this opportunity to prove your fitness, and you are here because your request was granted.

What happens when you go in?

The usual sequence of events will be as follows: The clerk (who is often the board stenographer) will introduce you to the chairman of the oral board, who will introduce you to the other members of the board. Acknowledge the introductions before you sit down. Do not be surprised if you find a microphone facing you or a stenotypist sitting by. Oral interviews are usually recorded in the event of an appeal or other review.

Usually the chairman of the board will open the interview by reviewing the highlights of your education and work experience from your application – primarily for the benefit of the other members of the board, as well as to get the material into the record. Do not interrupt or comment unless there is an error or significant misinterpretation; if that is the case, do not hesitate. But do not quibble about insignificant matters. Also, he will usually ask you some question about your education, experience or your present job – partly to get you to start talking and to establish the interviewing "rapport." He may start the actual questioning, or turn it over to one of the other members. Frequently, each member undertakes the questioning on a particular area, one in which he is perhaps most competent, so you can expect each member to participate in the examination. Because time is limited, you may also expect some rather abrupt switches in the direction the questioning takes, so do not be upset by it. Normally, a board member will not pursue a single line of questioning unless he discovers a particular strength or weakness.

After each member has participated, the chairman will usually ask whether any member has any further questions, then will ask you if you have anything you wish to add. Unless you are expecting this question, it may floor you. Worse, it may start you off on an extended, extemporaneous speech. The board is not usually seeking more information. The question is principally to offer you a last opportunity to present further qualifications or to indicate that you have nothing to add. So, if you feel that a significant qualification or characteristic has been overlooked, it is proper to point it out in a sentence or so. Do not compliment the board on the thoroughness of their examination – they have been sketchy, and you know it. If you wish, merely say, "No thank you, I have nothing further to add." This is a point where you can "talk yourself out" of a good impression or fail to present an important bit of information. Remember, *you close the interview yourself.*

The chairman will then say, "That is all, Mr. _____, thank you." Do not be startled; the interview is over, and quicker than you think. Thank him, gather your belongings and take your leave. Save your sigh of relief for the other side of the door.

How to put your best foot forward

Throughout this entire process, you may feel that the board individually and collectively is trying to pierce your defenses, seek out your hidden weaknesses and embarrass and confuse you. Actually, this is not true. They are obliged to make an appraisal of your qualifications for the job you are seeking, and they want to see you in your best light. Remember, they must interview all candidates and a non-cooperative candidate may become a failure in spite of their best efforts to bring out his qualifications. Here are 15 suggestions that will help you:

1) Be natural – Keep your attitude confident, not cocky

If you are not confident that you can do the job, do not expect the board to be. Do not apologize for your weaknesses, try to bring out your strong points. The board is interested in a positive, not negative, presentation. Cockiness will antagonize any board member and make him wonder if you are covering up a weakness by a false show of strength.

2) Get comfortable, but don't lounge or sprawl

Sit erectly but not stiffly. A careless posture may lead the board to conclude that you are careless in other things, or at least that you are not impressed by the importance of the occasion. Either conclusion is natural, even if incorrect. Do not fuss with your clothing, a pencil or an ashtray. Your hands may occasionally be useful to emphasize a point; do not let them become a point of distraction.

3) Do not wisecrack or make small talk

This is a serious situation, and your attitude should show that you consider it as such. Further, the time of the board is limited – they do not want to waste it, and neither should you.

4) Do not exaggerate your experience or abilities

In the first place, from information in the application or other interviews and sources, the board may know more about you than you think. Secondly, you probably will not get away with it. An experienced board is rather adept at spotting such a situation, so do not take the chance.

5) If you know a board member, do not make a point of it, yet do not hide it

Certainly you are not fooling him, and probably not the other members of the board. Do not try to take advantage of your acquaintanceship – it will probably do you little good.

6) Do not dominate the interview

Let the board do that. They will give you the clues – do not assume that you have to do all the talking. Realize that the board has a number of questions to ask you, and do not try to take up all the interview time by showing off your extensive knowledge of the answer to the first one.

7) Be attentive

You only have 20 minutes or so, and you should keep your attention at its sharpest throughout. When a member is addressing a problem or question to you, give him your undivided attention. Address your reply principally to him, but do not exclude the other board members.

8) Do not interrupt

A board member may be stating a problem for you to analyze. He will ask you a question when the time comes. Let him state the problem, and wait for the question.

9) Make sure you understand the question

Do not try to answer until you are sure what the question is. If it is not clear, restate it in your own words or ask the board member to clarify it for you. However, do not haggle about minor elements.

10) Reply promptly but not hastily

A common entry on oral board rating sheets is "candidate responded readily," or "candidate hesitated in replies." Respond as promptly and quickly as you can, but do not jump to a hasty, ill-considered answer.

11) Do not be peremptory in your answers

A brief answer is proper – but do not fire your answer back. That is a losing game from your point of view. The board member can probably ask questions much faster than you can answer them.

12) Do not try to create the answer you think the board member wants

He is interested in what kind of mind you have and how it works – not in playing games. Furthermore, he can usually spot this practice and will actually grade you down on it.

13) Do not switch sides in your reply merely to agree with a board member

Frequently, a member will take a contrary position merely to draw you out and to see if you are willing and able to defend your point of view. Do not start a debate, yet do not surrender a good position. If a position is worth taking, it is worth defending.

14) Do not be afraid to admit an error in judgment if you are shown to be wrong

    The board knows that you are forced to reply without any opportunity for careful consideration. Your answer may be demonstrably wrong. If so, admit it and get on with the interview.

15) Do not dwell at length on your present job

    The opening question may relate to your present assignment. Answer the question but do not go into an extended discussion. You are being examined for a *new* job, not your present one. As a matter of fact, try to phrase ALL your answers in terms of the job for which you are being examined.

Basis of Rating

    Probably you will forget most of these "do's" and "don'ts" when you walk into the oral interview room. Even remembering them all will not ensure you a passing grade. Perhaps you did not have the qualifications in the first place. But remembering them will help you to put your best foot forward, without treading on the toes of the board members.

    Rumor and popular opinion to the contrary notwithstanding, an oral board wants you to make the best appearance possible. They know you are under pressure – but they also want to see how you respond to it as a guide to what your reaction would be under the pressures of the job you seek. They will be influenced by the degree of poise you display, the personal traits you show and the manner in which you respond.

ABOUT THIS BOOK

    This book contains tests divided into Examination Sections. Go through each test, answering every question in the margin. At the end of each test look at the answer key and check your answers. On the ones you got wrong, look at the right answer choice and learn. Do not fill in the answers first. Do not memorize the questions and answers, but understand the answer and principles involved. On your test, the questions will likely be different from the samples. Questions are changed and new ones added. If you understand these past questions you should have success with any changes that arise. Tests may consist of several types of questions. We have additional books on each subject should more study be advisable or necessary for you. Finally, the more you study, the better prepared you will be. This book is intended to be the last thing you study before you walk into the examination room. Prior study of relevant texts is also recommended. NLC publishes some of these in our Fundamental Series. Knowledge and good sense are important factors in passing your exam. Good luck also helps. So now study this Passbook, absorb the material contained within and take that knowledge into the examination. Then do your best to pass that exam.

———

EXAMINATION SECTION

EXAMINATION SECTION
TEST 1

DIRECTIONS: Each question or incomplete statement is followed by several suggested answers or completions. Select the one that BEST answers the question or completes the statement. *PRINT THE LETTER OF THE CORRECT ANSWER IN THE SPACE AT THE RIGHT.*

1. A specialist is a physician who has restricted his or her practice to a given body system. Which of the statements below is FALSE concerning the various medical specialties? A(n)

    A. internist deals with diseases of the bones
    B. opthamologist deals with diseases of the eye
    C. dermatologist deals with diseases of the skin
    D. neurologist deals with diseases of the brain and nervous system

1.____

2. Alcohol has which of the following effects on the body? Alcohol

    A. causes blood vessels near the skin to constrict
    B. helps the body retain heat
    C. stimulates responses by the brain
    D. stimulates the secretion of acid in the stomach

2.____

3. The term hypertension refers to someone who

    A. has high blood pressure
    B. has overtaxed his muscular system
    C. has stomach ulcers
    D. does not deal effectively with stress

3.____

4. When a person exhibits neurotic behavior, he may

    A. act in a peculiar way or exhibit physical symptoms because of his response to anxiety
    B. hallucinate and perceive objects around him to be different than they really are
    C. perceive reality in such a distorted way that he may be unable to function properly
    D. exhibit two widely different personalities or extremely different moods

4.____

5. Gonorrhea, the MOST frequently reported venereal disease,

    A. has early symptoms that are usually more pronounced in women than in men
    B. may be diagnosed by a blood test and treated with injections of gamma globulin
    C. is normally transmitted through sexual intercourse
    D. is caused and transferred by a virus

5.____

6. Which organ of the body is responsible for the oxidation of alcohol into simpler products? The

    A. heart   B. liver   C. lungs   D. stomach

6.____

7. Ovulation USUALLY occurs in the human female   7.____

     A.   approximately five days before the end of the menstrual cycle
     B.   approximately halfway between menstrual cycles
     C.   during menstruation
     D.   approximately five days after the beginning of menstruation

8. Which one of the following behaviors on the part of parents could be damaging to developing positive emotional health in children?   8.____

     A.   Showing their love, support, and acceptance to their children
     B.   Listening carefully to what their children have to say
     C.   Setting no limits on what type of behaviors and actions are acceptable for their children
     D.   Teaching the child to share with others and to consider others

9. When treating a person for shock, you should   9.____

     A.   give the individual a stimulant to increase the blood pressure
     B.   make sure the individual is sitting up to prevent fainting
     C.   keep the individual warm and lying still
     D.   place a pillow or other soft object under the individual's head to elevate this portion of the body

10. Most people will FIRST feel some effects from drinking alcoholic beverages when the percentage of alcohol in the blood reaches   10.____

     A.   .02 to .05%   B.   .5 to .7%
     C.   1 to 2%   D.   .2 to .4%

11. Which drug below probably has the GREATEST tendency to be addictive?   11.____

     A.   Heroin   B.   Benzedrine
     C.   Phenobarbital   D.   Alcohol

12. It is important to apply a splint to a fractured limb before transporting a person because the splint will   12.____

     A.   relieve the pain by keeping the limb immobile
     B.   prevent the bones from growing together crookedly
     C.   allow for limited use of the limb
     D.   keep the bones immobile and prevent injury to muscles, blood vessels, and nerves

13. A person will never feel the intoxicating effects of alcohol if   13.____

     A.   the rate at which alcohol is absorbed into the blood is greater than the rate at which the body oxidizes the alcohol
     B.   the consumption of alcohol takes place slowly, but steadily
     C.   the rate at which alcohol is absorbed into the blood is equal to the rate at which the body oxidizes the alcohol
     D.   only beverages low in alcoholic content are consumed

14. Which of the following statements about the prevention and control of venereal disease is INCORRECT?   14.____

    A. If a person thinks he or she has been exposed to venereal disease, it is important to wait to see what symptoms develop before seeing a doctor.

    B. The probability of contracting venereal disease is greater when a person has many sexual partners.

    C. It is possible for venereal disease to be transmitted by kissing or by contact with open sores or broken skin.

    D. When a case of venereal disease is confirmed, it is important to discover the names of that person's sexual partner or partners.

15. The table below contains the basic information for Mr. Jones' diet on a daily basis. In addition, it is known that a reduction of 3,500 calories is required to lose one pound of fat. Using all this data, how many pounds would Mr. Jones lose in seven days?   15.____

Mr. Jones' basal metabolism	1600 cal/day
On his diet, Mr. Jones eats foods with a calorie content	1200 cal/day
Also on his diet, Mr. Jones has an exercise program in which he *burns up*	600 cal/day

_____ pound (s).

    A. Almost six   B. Two   C. One   D. Four

16. Which of the following is part of the male reproductive system?   16.____

    A. Fallopian tube   B. Vas deferens
    C. Cervix   D. Pineal gland

17. Under certain conditions, isometric exercise may be used as part of a fitness program to help develop   17.____

    A. strength   B. speed   C. endurance   D. flexibility

18. When considering the purchase of a health insurance policy, one should   18.____

    A. choose a policy that covers all routine costs
    B. avoid a policy that has a deductible clause
    C. choose a policy with the lowest premium cost
    D. choose a policy that covers the cost of medical services you can't afford

19. To aid yourself in developing positive emotional health, you should do all of the following EXCEPT   19.____

    A. attempt to resolve all problems by yourself and not not ask others for help
    B. use your own experiences as learning devices and modify your behavior accordingly
    C. develop a willingness to accept responsibility
    D. attempt to keep your body physically healthy

20. The PRIMARY purpose of Medicare is to help
    A. pay medical costs for the aged
    B. provide financial assistance to community health organizations
    C. pay medical costs of dependent children
    D. pay medical costs for the poor

20.____

21. A person who regularly takes narcotics commonly experiences all of the following EXCEPT
    A. reduced sexual drive or impotence
    B. constricted pupils
    C. diarrhea
    D. malnutrition

21.____

22. In the case of a severe burn that results in the blistering and charring of the skin, you should
    A. wash the area with soap and water to remove burned skin and prevent infection
    B. cover the burned area with a dry sterile dressing to reduce loss of body fluids
    C. remove fluid from blisters and cover with a clean sterile dressing
    D. cover the burned area with an ointment to reduce pain

22.____

23. Which drug or drug type in the list below can BEST be classified as a stimulant?
    A. Barbiturates   B. Amphetamines
    C. Alcohol   D. Opiates

23.____

24. The BEST emergency procedure to stop most cases of severe bleeding is to apply
    A. pressure directly over the wound
    B. a clean sterile bandage to the wound
    C. pressure at the closest pressure point
    D. a tourniquet

24.____

25. Some terms involving infectious disease are:
    I. Infection
    II. Invasion
    III. Incubation
What is the CORRECT order or sequence of these terms in regard to how an infectious disease affects the human body?
    A. II, I, III   B. I, II, III
    C. II, III, I   D. I, III, II

25.____

26. One of the procedures of CPR (cardio-pulmonary resuscitation) is external heart massage.
Which of the following statements about external heart massage is FALSE?
External heart massage
    A. is usually accompanied by mouth-to-mouth resuscitation
    B. squeezes the heart between the sternum and spine
    C. should only be given when there is no apparent carotid pulse
    D. should be given on a soft, unresistant surface to prevent injury to ribs

26.____

27. Which of the following is an effect of regular smoking?	27.____
    Smoking

    A. increases the number of stillbirths in pregnant women
    B. tends to make it more difficult for the blood to clot
    C. reduces the chances of developing a stomach ulcer
    D. increases the appetite and stimulates the sense of smell

28. The emergency treatment to be used on a child who has swallowed a strong corrosive	28.____
    substance should include all of the following EXCEPT

    A. treating the child for shock
    B. inducing vomiting
    C. calling a doctor or local hospital
    D. giving the child water or milk to drink

29. Carbon monoxide, one of the substances found in cigarette smoke, is thought to cause	29.____
    shortness of breath because

    A. it is a depressant on the respiratory system
    B. it leaves a deposit of tar in the lungs
    C. it reduces the oxygen-carrying capacity of the blood
    D. hot carbon monoxide tends to singe the lung surfaces

30. The BEST way to choose a family doctor is to	30.____

    A. look for a physician closest to home
    B. consult the phone directory for a list of available physicians
    C. ask your local hospital or medical society for recommendations
    D. look in the advertisement section of the newspaper

KEY (CORRECT ANSWERS)

1.	A		16.	B
2.	D		17.	A
3.	A		18.	D
4.	A		19.	A
5.	C		20.	A
6.	B		21.	B
7.	B		22.	B
8.	C		23.	B
9.	C		24.	C
10.	A		25.	C
11.	A		26.	D
12.	D		27.	A
13.	C		28.	B
14.	C		29.	C
15.	B		30.	C

TEST 2

DIRECTIONS: Each question or incomplete statement is followed by several suggested answers or completions. Select the one that BEST answers the question or completes the statement. *PRINT THE LETTER OF THE CORRECT ANSWER IN THE SPACE AT THE RIGHT.*

1. Which of the following physiological changes commonly occurs in women during pregnancy?
   The

   A. size of the heart is slightly reduced
   B. breasts increase in size
   C. position of the diaphragm is lowered
   D. breathing rate is lowered

   1._____

2. The MAIN difference between aerobic and anaerobic exercise is that

   A. aerobic exercise is less suited to older persons than is anaerobic exercise
   B. aerobic exercise involves rapid and vigorous movements, while anaerobic exercise involves rhythmic and more fluid movements
   C. in aerobic exercise sufficient oxygen is present, but in anaerobic exercise, there is an oxygen deficiency
   D. aerobic exercise should be done no more than once a week to be most effective, while anaerobic exercise should be done more often

   2._____

3. Cancer can BEST be defined as a(n)

   A. abnormal growth and spread of cells
   B. elevated white blood cell count
   C. viral infection
   D. fungus infection

   3._____

4. To understand emotional responses, you should realize that

   A. your emotions cannot result in sickness
   B. your emotional responses are like reflexes that involve no thinking
   C. your emotional responses are related to your personal values
   D. you were born with the emotions you have now

   4._____

5. Conception, or fertilization, in the human female

   A. requires implantation of the egg on the wall of the vagina
   B. requires one sperm to penetrate one egg
   C. takes place in the uterus
   D. takes place during menstruation

   5._____

6. The MAJOR importance of fiber in the diet is that it

   A. provides energy for the body
   B. is a source of important minerals
   C. is extremely easy to digest
   D. helps in normal elimination

   6._____

7. The incompatibility of the Rh blood factors in a pregnancy can be a problem when   7.____

     A. the mother is Rh positive and the father is Rh negative
     B. both the mother and father are Rh negative
     C. the mother is Rh negative and the baby is Rh positive
     D. both mother and baby are Rh negative

8. Which statement about vitamins is TRUE?   8.____

     A. The more vitamins you take, the more healthy your body will be.
     B. Some vitamins may be manufactured by the body.
     C. Vitamins are important sources of energy.
     D. Vitamins are a substitute for fats, proteins, and carbohydrates.

9. Below are listed some characteristics and symptoms of a common infectious disease: 9.____
     I. In the United States, its greatest incidence is among young people fifteen to nineteen years old.
     II. Symptoms may include fever, sore throat, nausea, and chills.
     III. A general weakness for three weeks to several months is common after the initial symptoms have passed.
     IV. A blood test can be used to diagnose the disease. From this information, you can diagnose this infectious disease as

     A. measles   B. mononucleosis
     C. hepatitis   D. pneumonia

10. Foods that are good sources of protein include   10.____

     A. fish, eggs, and cheese
     B. butter, margarine, and corn oil
     C. fruits and vegetables
     D. bread and cereal

11. An unborn human fetus receives nourishment through the   11.____

     A. amniotic fluid
     B. digestive system of the fetus
     C. lining of the uterus
     D. placenta

12. The MAJOR reason vegetarians must select a variety of foods is that   12.____

     A. vegetables are low in carbohydrates
     B. a wide variety of different enzymes is necessary in the digestive system
     C. eight essential amino acids are needed to build protein
     D. excesses of certain vitamins must be avoided

13. Which one of the following CANNOT be an infectious agent?   13.____

     A. Worms   B. Protozoa   C. Platelets   D. Fungus

14. The high consumption of foods that contain large amounts of saturated fats may represent a health hazard because these fats   14.____

    A. seem to increase the probability of developing cancer
    B. cause a build-up of fat-soluble vitamins in the body
    C. are thought to be a factor in heart disease
    D. accumulate in the liver and interfere with the production of bile

15. Which one of the following is considered to be a non-infectious disease?   15.____

    A. Pneumonia   B. Arthritis
    C. The common cold   D. Influenza

16. Defense mechanisms such as rationalization, repression, and escape   16.____

    A. represent responses that help reduce the stress of emotional conflict
    B. are signs of psychosis
    C. are effectively used when the emotional conflicts become overwhelming
    D. represent responses that help reduce the stress of emotional conflict

17. The endocrine glands serve an important function in the body by   17.____

    A. producing substances that carry nerve impulses
    B. producing hormones which regulate many body processes
    C. helping to regulate a person's genetic make-up
    D. releasing disease-fighting agents directly into the bloodstream

18. Which of the statements below is TRUE concerning cancer?   18.____

    A. A *pap smear* is an effective treatment for cancer.
    B. A lump in a woman's breast means she has cancer.
    C. Early diagnosis is important to cure cancer.
    D. Most skin cancers are fatal.

19. In any well-constructed weight-reducing diet, a person should   19.____

    A. only eat foods that contain no calories
    B. eliminate all favorite foods to reduce calorie intake
    C. strive for a weight loss of no more than one or two pounds per week
    D. reduce the amount of strenuous physical activity

20. Since syphilis is a serious venereal disease among young people, it is IMPORTANT to know that   20.____

    A. if left untreated even after many years, syphilis causes only minor physical damage
    B. syphilis is difficult to treat, even with antibiotics
    C. once a person is cured of syphilis, the body's immune system prevents that person from becoming reinfected
    D. the first symptom of the disease is often a sore or lesion in the genital region

21. The health hazards of being overweight include   21.____

    A. increased chances of becoming anemic
    B. severely reduced blood pressure
    C. increased chances of developing heart disease
    D. the likelihood of vitamin deficiencies

22. One of the changes that occurs in both boys and girls during puberty is   22.____

    A. improved physical coordination
    B. decreased hormone production
    C. increased amount of body hair
    D. reduced rate of growth

23. Which one of the following statements listed concerning a person's emotional health is   23.____
TRUE?

    A. Emotionally healthy people do not experience anxiety.
    B. Emotionally healthy people have no psychological needs.
    C. Emotional health is measured by a set of exact standards.
    D. Emotionally healthy people may avoid situations that will cause them to become anxious.

24. Antibodies, which help fight disease in the body, are   24.____

    A. proteins manufactured by the body's white cells that react against disease organisms or their toxins
    B. drugs, produced in other living things, which, when injected into the body, help kill disease organisms or their toxins
    C. living infectious agents that are used in vaccines to stimulate the body's immune response
    D. substances from outside the body that stimulate the body's immune response

25. The material found in cigarette smoke that contains the MOST carcinogens is   25.____

    A. tar   B. ammonia   C. ash   D. nicotine

26. The MAIN function of the digestive organ indicated by the arrow in the diagram below is   26.____

    A. absorption of essential nutrients
    B. absorption of water
    C. secretion of digestive enzymes
    D. secretion of hydrochloric acid

27. To reduce the likelihood of developing cardiovascular disease, one should   27.____

    A. keep busy working and only rarely relax
    B. eliminate exercise to avoid straining the heart
    C. eliminate or reduce cigarette smoking
    D. eat plenty of butter, milk, eggs, and cheese

28. When people smoke, the nicotine in tobacco tends to cause a(n)   28._____

   A.   sharp decrease in a person's blood pressure
   B.   constricting of the blood vessels
   C.   decrease in the heartbeat
   D.   increase in temperature in the fingers and toes

29. When purchasing a prescription drug, why should you ask the pharmacist whether the   29._____
drug has a generic equivalent?
Generic equivalent drugs

   A.   are more pure than the brand-name drug
   B.   usually have fewer bad side effects than the brand-name drug
   C.   are designed to give you a higher dosage
   D.   are usually less expensive than brand-name drugs

30. In any weight-reducing diet, the nutritional calorie is of interest to the dieter.   30._____
The nutritional calorie is

   A.   found in larger amounts in protein than in any other basic nutrient
   B.   a measure of the amount of body fat
   C.   found in everything we eat or drink
   D.   considered as a unit that measures the amount of fuel entering the body

_____

KEY (CORRECT ANSWERS)

1.	B	16.	A
2.	B	17.	B
3.	A	18.	C
4.	C	19.	C
5.	B	20.	D
6.	D	21.	C
7.	C	22.	C
8.	B	23.	D
9.	B	24.	A
10.	A	25.	A
11.	D	26.	B
12.	A	27.	C
13.	C	28.	B
14.	C	29.	D
15.	B	30.	D

_____

EXAMINATION SECTION
TEST 1

DIRECTIONS: Each question or incomplete statement is followed by several suggested answers or completions. Select the one that BEST answers the question or completes the statement. *PRINT THE LETTER OF THE CORRECT ANSWER IN THE SPACE AT THE RIGHT.*

1. Which one of the following is classified as a fissure of the brain?　　　1._____

    A. Maxillary plexuses　　　　　　B. Periphlebitis
    C. Visceral cleavage　　　　　　　D. Parieto-occipital sulcus

2. Paralysis of corresponding parts on two sides of the body is known as　　　2._____

    A. diplegia　　　B. hemiplegia　　　C. monoplegia　　　D. hemiparesis

3. Muscular dystrophy is a condition in which　　　3._____

    A. the cause is known
    B. there is apparently no hereditary transmission
    C. several members of the family are often affected in the same manner
    D. the juvenile type is rarely found in boys

4. Tachycardia is a condition of the _____ system.　　　4._____

    A. skeletal　　　　　　　　　　　B. endocrine
    C. circulatory　　　　　　　　　　D. digestive

5. Which one of the following diseases involves the lymph nodes and has a poor prognosis?　　　5._____

    A. Colitis　　　　　　　　　　　　B. Ileitis
    C. Lordosis　　　　　　　　　　　D. Hodgkin's disease ·

6. Of the following diseases, the one that is NOT directly attributable to a specific vitamin deficiency is　　　6._____

    A. scurvy　　　B. beriberi　　　C. tularemia　　　D. pellagra

7. The three bones known as the *hammer, anvil,* and *stirrup* are found in the human　　　7._____

    A. nose　　　B. knee　　　C. ear　　　D. elbow

8. Of the following body functions, the one performed by the white blood cells is　　　8._____

    A. carrying carbon dioxide to the lungs
    B. destroying invading bacteria
    C. carrying food particles to the cells
    D. destroying old red blood corpuscles

9. Of the following, the word *dyspnea* is MOST closely associated with　　　9._____

    A. bronchial asthma　　　　　　B. meningitis
    C. rickets　　　　　　　　　　　D. synovitis

10. A disease characterized by tonic spasms in the voluntarily moved muscles is   10.____

    A. osteomyelitis   B. otomycosis
    C. pleuralgia   D. myotonia congenita

11. With which one of the following is the term *aura* MOST commonly associated?   11.____

    A. Psycho-motor seizures   B. Petit mal seizures
    C. Grand mal seizures   D. Laryngospasm

12. *A short lapse of consciousness and a sudden momentary pause in conversation or movement* is MOST suggestive of   12.____

    A. nephrosis   B. autism
    C. Friedreich's ataxia   D. petit mal seizure

13. Which one of the following diseases usually has a very poor prognosis?   13.____

    A. Hodgkin's disease   B. Slipped epiphsys
    C. Cerebral palsy   D. Eczema

14. Mononucleosis is an abnormal condition of the   14.____

    A. blood   B. liver   C. nerves   D. colon

15. Increased thirst, increased urination, loss of weight, and general fatigue are common symptoms of   15.____

    A. arthrogryposis   B. diabetes
    C. hepatitis   D. arthritis

16. Dementia praecox is now commonly called _____ reaction.   16.____

    A. schizophrenic   B. depressive
    C. manic   D. obsessive

17. Which one of the following is a disease of the ear?   17.____

    A. Ostitis   B. Otitis
    C. Omphalitis   D. Ophthalmia

18. Glomerulonephritis is a disease of the   18.____

    A. heart   B. stomach   C. kidney   D. larynx

19. Which one of the following is the disease that would MOST likely impair the ability to ambulate?   19.____

    A. Diabetes   B. Colitis
    C. Bronchiectasis   D. Spina bifida

20. The lay term *hunchback* is synonymous with   20.____

    A. kyphosis   B. scoliosis
    C. torticollis   D. spondylolisthesis

21. Which one of the following diseases involves a malformation of the heart?   21.____

    A. Hydrocele   B. Tetralogy of Fallot
    C. Myasthenia gravis   D. Lordosis

22. Of the following, the disease which would be included under the general classification *orthopedic* is   22.____

    A. lupus erythematosus   B. lymphedema
    C. Osgood-Schlatter's   D. opthalmospasm

23. Of the following cardiac classifications, the one the teacher would be LEAST likely to encounter is   23.____

    A. 4A   B. 3C   C. 4E   D. 2C

24. The name Cooley is MOST closely associated with a form of   24.____

    A. anemia   B. dystrophy
    C. asthma   D. cerebral palsy

25. Chorea is a disease of the _____ system.   25.____

    A. digestive   B. respiratory
    C. circulatory   D. nervous

26. Rickets results from a lack of calcium and of vitamin   26.____

    A. A   B. C   C. D   D. E

27. Recommended foods to alleviate rickets should include   27.____

    A. leafy vegetables, meat, fruits
    B. bread, cereals, dried beans
    C. tomatoes, apricots, green vegetables
    D. canned salmon, liver, whole milk

28. Which one of the following diseases is ALWAYS congenital?   28.____

    A. Cerebral palsy   B. Osteogenesis imperfecta
    C. Rheumatoid arthritis   D. Pericarditis

29. Of the following, which condition represents a disturbance of the neuro-muscular system frequently accompanied by perceptual difficulties?   29.____

    A. Perthe's disease   B. Cerebral palsy
    C. Spina bifida   D. Talipes

30. The following symptoms are noted in a group of children: enlargement of the calf muscles, difficulty in raising arms, afflicted shoulder and face muscles, waddling gait. The children are *probably* suffering from   30.____

    A. spina bifida   B. polio
    C. muscular dystrophy   D. Perthe's disease

31. Of the following diseases, which one is hereditary?   31.____

    A. Scoliosis   B. Osteomyelitis
    C. Hemophilia   D. Chorea

32. In which one of the following diseases is overweight frequently a concomitant?   32.____

    A. Pott's disease   B. Epilepsy
    C. Slipped epiphysis   D. Coxa vara

33. Hyperactivity is MOST apt to be observed in children who have   33.____

    A. muscular dystrophy   B. brain damage
    C. ileitis   D. rheumatic fever

34. Three broad categories of physical disabilities–orthopedic, cardiac, and chronic–are   34.____
often used for convenience in classifying children in health conservation classes.
The group below which BEST fits into the category of *chronic* is

    A. rheumatic fever, muscular dystrophy, kyphosis
    B. nephrosis, colitis, hepatitis
    C. Friedreich's ataxia, osteomyelitis, torticollis
    D. rickets, chorea, arthogryposis

35. The one of the following diseases which is the *leading* cause of death in the 10- to 15-   35.____
year age group is

    A. cancer   B. poliomyelitis
    C. diabetes   D. rheumatic fever

36. The one of the following which would MOST likely be a result of untreated syphilis is   36.____

    A. paresis   B. phlebitis   C. carcinoma   D. silicosis

37. The one of the following which is MOST likely to be used in establishing a diagnosis of   37.____
epilepsy is a(n)

    A. electrocardiogram   B. spinal x-ray
    C. fluoroscopic examination   D. electroencephalogram

38. The pathology of diabetes involves the failure of the body to produce an adequate supply   38.____
of

    A. sugar   B. carbohydrates   C. insulin   D. salt

39. The one of the following statements which is TRUE about diabetes is that   39.____

    A. it can generally be cured if medical orders are followed
    B. it can generally be kept under control but not cured
    C. it is an infectious disease
    D. blindness is an inevitable result of it

40. Scurvy is caused by a deficiency of vitamin   40.____

    A. A   B. B   C. C   D. K

41. The one of the following diseases which is covered by benefits under the Worker's   41.____
Compensation Law is

    A. syphilis   B. diabetes
    C. poliomyelitis   D. silicosis

42. The one of the following vitamins which is used as an aid in coagulating blood is vitamin   42.____

    A. A   B. B   C. C   D. K

43. The one of the following statements which is TRUE of progressive muscular dystrophy is that   43.____

    A. it is transmitted to the male children through the mother
    B. the male is the carrier of the disease
    C. the brain is primarily affected because of a lack of blood supply
    D. it is caused by a nutritional deficiency in the ante-partum period

44. If a patient is repeatedly admitted to the hospital because of a series of mishaps in which he has suffered broken bones, the one of the following which is MOST likely to be true is that he is   44.____

    A. a rigid person   B. a diabetic
    C. malingering   D. accident-prone

45. The one of the following groups of illnesses which is known to be caused by bacteria is _____ diseases.   45.____

    A. mental   B. acute infectious
    C. nutritional   D. degenerative

46. The one of the following with which Hodgkin's disease is commonly associated is   46.____

    A. neurasthenia   B. meningitis
    C. poliomyelitis   D. cancer

47. The one of the following diseases in which the determination of the sedimentation rate is important for diagnostic purposes is   47.____

    A. rheumatic heart disease
    B. congenital heart disease
    C. hypertensive heart disease
    D. diabetes

48. The one of the following disease classifications which would include spinal meningitis is   48.____

    A. cancer or tumor
    B. nutritional disease
    C. acute infectious disease
    D. focal or local infection

49. The one of the following diseases which may cause visual impairment and blindness is   49.____

    A. ringworm   B. osteomyelitis
    C. poliomyelitis   D. diabetes

50. The one of the following which is NOT an anesthetic is   50.____

    A. cholesterol   B. nitrous oxide
    C. sodium pentothal   D. procaine

KEY (CORRECT ANSWERS)

1.	D	11.	C	21.	B	31.	C	41.	D
2.	A	12.	D	22.	C	32.	C	42.	D
3.	C	13.	A	23.	A	33.	B	43.	A
4.	C	14.	A	24.	A	34.	B	44.	D
5.	D	15.	B	25.	D	35.	D	45.	B
6.	C	16.	A	26.	C	36.	A	46.	D
7.	C	17.	B	27.	D	37.	D	47.	A
8.	B	18.	C	28.	B	38.	C	48.	C
9.	A	19.	D	29.	B	39.	B	49.	D
10.	D	20.	A	30.	C	40.	C	50.	A

TEST 2

DIRECTIONS: Each question or incomplete statement is followed by several suggested answers or completions. Select the one that BEST answers the question or completes the statement. *PRINT THE LETTER OF THE CORRECT ANSWER IN THE SPACE AT THE RIGHT.*

1. The one of the following which is MOST likely to be an occupational disease is   1.____

    A. cancer   B. cerebral hemorrhage
    C. septicemia   D. arsenic poisoning

2. The one of the following which is a nutritional disease is   2.____

    A. tuberculosis   B. rickets
    C. bubonic plague   D. typhoid fever

3. Tachycardia is a condition o the _____ system.   3.____

    A. skeletal   B. endocrine
    C. circulatory   D. digestive

4. Which one of the following diseases involves the lymph nodes and has a poor prognosis?   4.____

    A. Colitis   B. Ileitis
    C. Lordosis   D. Hodgkin's disease

5. Which of the following diseases has yielded to chemotherapeutic treatment in recent years?   5.____

    A. Multiple sclerosis   B. Tuberculosis
    C. Diabetes   D. Scleroderma

6. The MOST satisfactory results in the treatment of epilepsy have been obtained through the use of   6.____

    A. vitamins   B. diet   C. drugs   D. exercise

7. In former years, all members of the family of a child with a communicable disease were quarantined.   7.____
    At the present time, the child's siblings may attend school unless the disease in question is

    A. diphtheria   B. whooping cough
    C. mumps   D. ringworm

8. The CHIEF purpose of the Snellen test is   8.____

    A. diagnosis   B. screening
    C. placement   D. prognosis

9. During the daily health observation period, the teacher notices that a child has evidence of pediculosis.   9.____
    The teacher should

    A. isolate the child from the group
    B. send for a parent and explain the seriousness of the situation

17

C. give a talk on the subject to the class
D. refer the child to the principal for possible exclusion

10. Which one of the following diseases may result in brain damage?   10.____

    A. Poliomyelitis   B. Lymphadenoma
    C. Spondylitis   D. Encephalitis

11. A disease usually characterized by frequent vomiting and cramps is   11.____

    A. colitis   B. bronchitis
    C. myocarditis   D. empyemia

12. A lateral curvature of the spine is characteristic of   12.____

    A. scoliosis   B. lordosis   C. hyphosis   D. stenosis

13. Which of the following is one of the great dangers of many forms of anemia?   13.____

    A. Brain deterioration   B. Secondary infection
    C. Mental deficiency   D. Bleeding

14. A cleft of the vertebral column with meningeal protrusion is characteristic of   14.____

    A. Sprengel's deformity   B. scoliosis
    C. coxa vara   D. spina bifida

15. When correctly used, the term *allergen* refers to   15.____

    A. a person who is allergic
    B. an antihistamine medication
    C. a substance which produces allergy
    D. the tendency to inherit an allergy

16. Which of the following is congenital?   16.____

    A. Meningitis   B. Gastroenteritis
    C. Chronic bronchitis   D. Osteogenesis imperfecta

17. Spasm is a common characteristic of   17.____

    A. slipped epiphysis   B. otitis
    C. muscular dystrophy   D. asthma

18. Which one of the following is MOST likely to be associated with production of large quantities of mucous?   18.____

    A. Kyphosis   B. Bronchiectasis
    C. Lymphodenoma   D. Thyroid deficiency

19. Poor bladder control is MOST frequently associated with   19.____

    A. rheumatic fever   B. hemophilia
    C. club foot   D. torticollis

20. Excessive accumulation of cerebrospinal fluid within the skull is usually characterized as   20.____

    A. mongolism   B. microcephaly
    C. macrocephaly   D. hydrocephaly

21. Cerebral palsy is a term applied to a group of conditions having in common   21.____

    A. hereditary malformation
    B. retarded mentality
    C. microcephalic appearance
    D. disorders of muscular control

22. Which one of the following conditions is caused by the inflammation of the lower part of the intestine?   22.____

    A. Pyelitis   B. Transverse myelitis
    C. Regional ileitis   D. Hepatitis

23. In contrast with former treatment methods that called for intramuscular injections, oral medication is now frequently provided for treating   23.____

    A. diabetes   B. colitis
    C. thyroiditis   D. myelitis

24. A child who has cerebral palsy has difficulty in keeping his paper on his desk. Which one of the following materials should his teacher provide to help him?   24.____

    A. A thick piece of oaktag   B. A paperweight
    C. Masking tape   D. A set of tacks

25. A bone fracture which is in the process of healing will call for greater intake of   25.____

    A. vitamin B complex   B. folic acid
    C. vitamins D and C   D. vitamins A and K

26. Antihistamines are often used in treating   26.____

    A. allergies   B. anemias
    C. glandular fevers   D. adrenal hemorrhages

27. A cardiac child classified as 4E would be MOST apt to   27.____

    A. be placed in a health conservation class
    B. receive home instruction
    C. be placed in a regular class with limited physical activity
    D. be placed in a regular class following a short stay in a special class

28. An underweight child with a cardiac condition should be encouraged to   28.____

    A. add candy to his diet
    B. add carbohydrates such as bread and milk desserts to his diet
    C. maintain weight below normal since this insures a margin of safety should illness occur
    D. increase his intake of fluids and salt

29. Which one of the following involves the degeneration of parts of the brain, or spinal chord, or both?   29.____

    A. Schizophrenia   B. Spina bifida
    C. Multiple sclerosis   D. Pott's disease

30. Of the following, the disability with the BEST prognosis is   30.____

    A. Cooley's anemia   B. encephalitis
    C. hemophilia   D. slipped epiphyses

31. Infectious mononucleosis is also known as   31.____

    A. Hodgkin's disease   B. glandular fever
    C. chorea   D. bronchiectasis

32. Which one of the following is non-inflammatory?   32.____

    A. Cystitis   B. Nephritis
    C. Nephrosis   D. Pyelitis

33. Idiopathic epilepsy may be BEST characterized as a condition which   33.____

    A. is of unknown origin
    B. is a result of some trauma
    C. is not amenable to treatment
    D. may be safely ignored

34. Which one of the following conditions is characterized by loss of weight, sleeplessness, irritability, and bulging eyes?   34.____

    A. Tuberculosis   B. Overactive thyroid
    C. Myasthenia gravis   D. Frederick's ataxia

35. Cardiac involvement may result from a previous acute, infectious disease. The disease referred to is   35.____

    A. streptococcus sore throat   B. measles
    C. uremia   D. enteric fever

36. A type of facial paralysis due to a neuritis of the facial nerve in the Fallopian canal is called   36.____

    A. Paget's disease   B. Bell's palsy
    C. endocarditis   D. encephalitis

37. A slipped epiphysis occurs MOST frequently in   37.____

    A. early adolescence   B. late adolescence
    C. pre-adolescence   D. early childhood

38. An electroencephalogram would NOT ordinarily be used in connection with   38.____

    A. epilepsy   B. ataxia   C. pyelitis   D. meningitis

39. Which of the following is characterized by lifeless muscle?   39.____

    A. Pott's disease   B. Flaccid paralysis
    C. Scoliosis   D. Colitis

40. The psychologist's report on a child states that he suffers from aphasia. Aphasia is a(n)   40.____

    A. impairment of the ability to use or understand spoken language
    B. disturbance of muscular coordination

C. neurotic reaction characterized by intense fear
D. inability consciously to recall events or personal identity

41. Which one of the following BEST defines *a suffix of nouns denoting a morbid condition of growth*?   41.____

    A. Oma   B. Itis   C. Osis   D. Omy

42. The formation of an artificial anus in the anterior abdominal wall or loin is known as a(n)   42.____

    A. anuria   B. achondroplasia
    C. colostomy   D. plastogene

43. Carpus, ethmoid, and coccyx are   43.____

    A. arteries   B. bones   C. enzymes   D. ligaments

44. Inflammation of the intestinal tract is known as   44.____

    A. enteritis   B. hepatitis
    C. glomerulonephritis   D. rhinitis

45. For the past twenty years, the leading cause of death in children has been   45.____

    A. rheumatic fever   B. poliomyelitis
    C. cancer   D. heart disease

46. Of the following, which one is the MOST frequent cause of long-term crippling conditions in children?   46.____

    A. Infections   B. Congenital defects
    C. Metabolic disturbances   D. Unknown causes

47. Which one of the following statements concerning rheumatic fever and heart disease is CORRECT?   47.____

    A. All children who have rheumatic fever will have heart disease.
    B. Some children who have had rheumatic fever will have heart disease.
    C. No children who have had rheumatic fever will have heart disease.
    D. All children with heart disease have had rheumatic fever.

48. Polyarthritis is sometimes used as a synonym for   48.____

    A. acute rheumatic fever   B. arthrochondritis
    C. multiple sclerosis   D. polyneuritis

49. Pfeiffer's disease, glandular fever, and infectious mononucleosis are all   49.____

    A. the same disease
    B. non-communicable diseases
    C. characterized by a decrease in abnormal mononuclear cells
    D. the result of an intestinal virus

50. Prolongation of the blood clotting time results from a deficiency of vitamin   50.____

    A. B_2 B. K   C. E   D. D

KEY (CORRECT ANSWERS)

1.	D	11.	A	21.	D	31.	B	41.	A
2.	B	12.	A	22.	C	32.	C	42.	C
3.	C	13.	B	23.	A	33.	A	43.	B
4.	D	14.	D	24.	C	34.	B	44.	A
5.	B	15.	C	25.	C	35.	A	45.	D
6.	C	16.	C	26.	A	36.	B	46.	B
7.	A	17.	D	27.	B	37.	A	47.	B
8.	B	18.	C	28.	B	38.	C	48.	A
9.	D	19.	A	29.	C	39.	B	49.	A
10.	D	20.	D	30.	D	40.	A	50.	B

TEST 3

DIRECTIONS: Each question or incomplete statement is followed by several suggested answers or completions. Select the one that BEST answers the question or completes the statement. *PRINT THE LETTER OF THE CORRECT ANSWER IN THE SPACE AT THE RIGHT.*

1. Of the following, the one which is NOT a symptom of shock is a   1._____

   A. cool, clammy skin   B. weak pulse
   C. flushed face   D. feeling of weakness

2. It is INCORRECT to state that the procedure of exercise that causes fatigue is   2._____

   A. sarcolactic acid   B. acid potassium phosphate
   C. carbon dioxide   D. glycogen

3. Of the following diseases or eruptions, the one which is non-communicable is   3._____

   A. ringworm   B. chicken pox
   C. pink eye   D. eczema

4. The so-called *fuel* foods used by the body are largely made up of   4._____

   A. vitamins   B. fats
   C. proteins   D. carbohydrates

5. The type of wound resulting from a floor burn is known as a(n)   5._____

   A. laceration   B. abrasion   C. incision   D. puncture

6. Of the following foods, the one *generally* considered to be RICHEST in minerals is   6._____

   A. fruit   B. pastry   C. cereal   D. meat

7. The pressure point MOST effective in controlling arterial bleeding of the forearm is located   7._____

   A. near the wrist
   B. near the elbow
   C. on the outer surface of the upper arm halfway between the shoulder and the elbow
   D. behind the inner end of the collarbone

8. According to the American Red Cross, carbon monoxide causes death by   8._____

   A. combining more readily with the red blood cells than oxygen does and thus depriving the body of oxygen
   B. destroying the red blood cells
   C. searing the air sacs of the lungs and preventing oxygen from entering the blood
   D. paralyzing the muscles that function in respiration

9. In the event of an emergency need for an ambulance, we should FIRST call the   9._____

   A. police   B. hospital
   C. health department   D. fire department

10. A direct blow upon a muscle produces a   10._____

    A. sprain   B. fracture   C. contusion   D. strain

11. The Health Department reports that, of the following, the cause of the GREATEST num-   11.____
ber of deaths in New York was

    A. accidents   B. heart disease
    C. cancer   D. diabetes

12. Upon discovering two members of the center smoking cigarettes on a stairway, you   12.____
should

    A. take them to an exit and make certain they leave the building
    B. tell them to put out the lighted cigarettes and, in the future, to step outside the
        building to smoke
    C. warn them that smoking is forbidden and they are liable to arrest
    D. None of the above

13. Congenital malformation of the brain is often associated with   13.____

    A. hydrocephaly   B. myelitis
    C. varicella   D. lupus erythematosus

14. The use of an electroencephalogram *usually* proves MOST valuable in the diagnosis of   14.____

    A. epilepsy   B. osteoma   C. lordosis   D. nephritis

15. Incontinence is MOST often an accompanying symptom of   15.____

    A. spina bifida   B. lordosis
    C. Friedreich's ataxia   D. Hodgkin's disease

16. Of the following, the MOST frequently observed preliminary indication of illness among   16.____
children is

    A. fever   B. listlessness
    C. skin rash   D. coughing

17. Inflammation of the intestinal tract is known as   17.____

    A. enteritis   B. hepatitis
    C. glomerulonephritis   D. rhinitis

18. Which one of the following conditions is CORRECTLY paired with an associated disabil-   18.____
ity often found as a secondary defect?

    A. Cerebral palsy - hearing defect
    B. Chorea - visual defect
    C. Perthe's disease - speech defect
    D. Torticollis - poor coordination

19. In which one of the following pairs is it MOST difficult to arrive at a differential diagnosis?   19.____

    A. Encephalitis - meningitis
    B. Aphasia - brain damage
    C. Poliomyelitis - muscular dystrophy
    D. Hydrocephalia - microcephalia

20. Abnormal brain wave discharges are MOST characteristic of   20.____

    A. diabetes   B. epilepsy   C. herpes   D. Hansen's disease

21. Polyarthritis is sometimes used as a synonym for   21.____

    A. acute rheumatic fever   B. arthrochondritis
    C. multiple sclerosis   D. polyneuritis

22. Pfeiffer's disease, glandular fever, and infectious mononucleosis are all   22.____

    A. the same disease
    B. non-communicable diseases
    C. characterized by a decrease in abnormal mononuclear cells
    D. the result of an intestinal virus

23. Prolongation of the blood clotting time results from a deficiency of vitamin   23.____

    A. B_2 B. K   C. E   D. D

24. Rheumatic fever may affect the body in all of the following ways EXCEPT by   24.____

    A. attacking the connective tissues of the body
    B. scarring the heart valves
    C. causing inflammation of the inner lining of the heart
    D. forming a clot of blood within the heart

25. A pupil who has been excluded from school because of scarlet fever may be readmitted   25.____
upon presentation of a note from the

    A. school nurse   B. department of health
    C. family physician   D. any of the above

26. In regard to polio immunity, all of the following statements are correct EXCEPT: 26.____

    A. Both the gamma globulin and the Salk vaccine protect against three known types of polio virus
    B. Gamma globulin is a mixture of antibodies against polio, while the Salk vaccine is a vaccination in which mild forms of the viruses are given
    C. The Salk vaccine is designed to give longer acquired immunity than the gamma globulin
    D. Gamma globulin is obtained only from the blood of persons who have recovered from polio

27. All of the following terms are associated with cancer EXCEPT   27.____

    A. scotoma   B. carcinoma   C. sarcoma   D. myeloma

28. Hemolytic streptococci are associated with all of the following EXCEPT   28.____

    A. septic sore throat   B. rheumatic fever
    C. scarlet fever   D. tuberculosis

29. All of the following statements concerning viruses are correct EXCEPT: 29.____

    A. Viruses are harder to kill than ordinary bacteria.

B. Viruses depend upon living cells for food.
C. Virus cultures can be set up with surviving cells.
D. Most of the antibiotics destroy viruses.

30. Of the following diseases, the one caused by protozoa is   30.____

    A. amebic dysentary   B. trichinosis
    C. hookworm   D. botulism

31. All of the following statements concerning epilepsy are correct EXCEPT: 31.____

    A. Seizures in about 50% of children with this condition can be controlled
    B. The correlation of epilepsy with mental retardation is relatively high
    C. The incidence of epilepsy is higher than that of polio
    D. Encephalographs have proved helpful in the diagnosis of epileptic seizures

32. All of the following associations are correct EXCEPT: 32.____

    A. William Menninger - heart surgery
    B. Elie Metchnikoff - function of white blood cells in engulfing and destroying bacteria
    C. Joseph Lister - use of antiseptics in surgery
    D. Alexander Fleming - effect of pencillium on growth bacteria

33. A person suffering from heterophoria may find that because of his condition,   33.____

    A. he is not able to walk rapidly without distress
    B. his reflexes have become slower
    C. his eyes have a tendency to turn away from the position of binocular vision
    D. he has difficulty in hearing high pitch sounds

34. Bell's palsy usually affects the   34.____

    A. abdominal area   B. chest
    C. lower extremities   D. facial area

35. All of the following associations are correct EXCEPT: 35.____

    A. Histology - science which deals with tissues
    B. Pathology - science which deals with the nature of disease
    C. Cytology - science which deals with cells
    D. Geomedicine - science which deals with old age and its diseases

36. All of the following are symptoms of disorders of the circulatory system EXCEPT   36.____

    A. dyspnea   B. hypertension   C. enteritis   D. cyanosis

37. The grouping of types of human blood is based upon the   37.____

    A. platelets   B. red corpuscles
    C. white corpuscles   D. thrombocytes

38. A vaccine is introduced into the body PRIMARILY to   38.____

    A. kill the causative organism
    B. stimulate the growth of specific antibodies
    C. inhibit the growth of the causative organism
    D. produce bacteriostasis

39. All of the following are recommended by the National Foot Health Council for children's shoes EXCEPT: 39.____

    A. Since the normal foot is springy and acts as a shock absorber, rubber-soled shoes are preferred to leather-soled shoes
    B. A counter of leather around the heel is preferable to any other material
    C. Shoes should be narrow at the top of the heel, yet wide enough at the base to provide pivoting room for the broad base of the heel bone
    D. A cloth lining over the toes should be provided to absorb moisture

40. All of the following advances in medicine occurred during the last fifty years EXCEPT the   40.____

    A. discovery that malignant cells can live without oxygen
    B. regulation by vitamin C of the rate at which cholesterol is formed
    C. use of typhoid fever vaccine for cases of encephalitis
    D. conversion of normal cells into cancer cells in test tubes

41. The one of the following which is MOST frequently the cause of cerebral palsy is   41.____

    A. an infectious disease   B. a birth injury
    C. a hereditary defect   D. poor nutrition

42. The one of the following conditions which is due to dysfunction of the thyroid gland is   42.____

    A. cholecystitis   B. cretinism
    C. congenital syphilis   D. epilepsy

43. Enuresis is MOST frequently a symptom of   43.____

    A. kidney infection   B. emotional problems
    C. poor personal hygiene   D. carelessness

44. The one of the following which is MOST frequently used in establishing a diagnosis of epilepsy is a(n)   44.____

    A. electroencephalogram   B. complete blood count
    C. electrocardiogram   D. glucose tolerance test

45. The one of the following which is NOT infectious is   45.____

    A. pulmonary tuberculosis   B. poliomyelitis
    C. syphilis   D. muscular dystrophy

46. For the past twenty years, the leading cause of death in children has been   46.____

    A. rheumatic fever   B. poliomyelitis
    C. cancer   D. heart disease

47. Of the following, which one is the MOST frequent cause of long-term crippling conditions in children?   47.____

    A. Infections   B. Congenital defects
    C. Metabolic disturbances   D. Unknown causes

48. Which one of the following statements concerning rheumatic fever and heart disease is CORRECT?   48.____

    A. All children who have rheumatic fever will have heart disease.
    B. Some children who have had rheumatic fever will have heart disease.
    C. No children who have had rheumatic fever will have heart disease.
    D. All children with heart disease have had rheumatic fever.

49. Of the following, which orthopedic disability gives rise to special educational placement of the LARGEST number of children?   49.____

    A. Slipped epiphysis   B. Multiple sclerosis
    C. Lordosis   D. Otitis

50. A disease in which the muscles appear to be replaced with fatty tissue is   50.____

    A. epiphysitis   B. kyphosis
    C. muscular dystrophy   D. Still's disease

KEY (CORRECT ANSWERS)

1.	C	11.	A	21.	A	31.	B	41.	B
2.	D	12.	B	22.	A	32.	A	42.	B
3.	D	13.	A	23.	B	33.	C	43.	B
4.	D	14.	A	24.	D	34.	D	44.	A
5.	B	15.	A	25.	B	35.	D	45.	D
6.	A	16.	B	26.	D	36.	C	46.	D
7.	D	17.	A	27.	A	37.	B	47.	B
8.	C	18.	A	28.	D	38.	B	48.	B
9.	A	19.	B	29.	D	39.	A	49.	A
10.	C	20.	B	30.	A	40.	A	50.	C

EXAMINATION SECTION
TEST 1

DIRECTIONS: Each question or incomplete statement is followed by several suggested answers or completions. Select the one that BEST answers the question or completes the statement. *PRINT THE LETTER OF THE CORRECT ANSWER IN THE SPACE AT THE RIGHT.*

1. Normally, upon exposure to air, blood clots form within _____ minutes.

   A. 30 seconds to two   B. three to ten
   C. ten to fifteen   D. fifteen to thirty

   1.____

2. The red blood cells of the body are produced in the

   A. spongy area of the long bones, in the ribs, and in the vertebrae
   B. ends of the long bones and the spleen
   C. liver and the flat bones
   D. pancreas and the liver

   2.____

3. All of the following statements are correct EXCEPT:

   A. The figures used for the recording of blood pressure represent in millimeters the height of a column of mercury in the sphygmomanometer.
   B. In high blood pressure cases, progressive damage to the blood vessels takes place, whereas hypertension is limited to harder than normal work by the heart to pump the same amount of blood around to the tissues.
   C. In the recording of blood pressure, the larger figure represents the maximum pressure in the arteries with each heart beat.
   D. The smaller figure in the recording of an individual's blood pressure registers the minimum pressure between heart beats.

   3.____

4. The physician can actually see the arteries and veins at work when he

   A. measures the pressure of the walls of the blood vessels
   B. uses the ophthalmoscope in examining the eyes
   C. applies a fluoroscope in examining a patient
   D. uses the electrocardiograph

   4.____

5. The blood-clotting process in the body is started by the breaking up of

   A. plasma   B. platelets
   C. white blood cells   D. red blood cells

   5.____

6. The condition that impairs the elasticity and function of the blood vessel walls and reduces the volume of blood that may pass through the afflicted arteries is

   A. hypertension   B. vascular occlusion
   C. high blood pressure   D. hardening of the arteries

   6.____

7. All of the following statements are correct EXCEPT:

   A. There is more limited mobility of the big toe of the foot compared to that of the thumb on the hand.

   7.____

B.   The foot bones are held together in such a way as to form springy lengthwise and crosswise arches.
C.   The much greater solidity of the big toe as compared to the fingers on the hand help the foot to support body weight.
D.   The phalanges of the foot are relatively more important than those of the hand and have a greater role in the functioning of the foot than those in the hand.

8.   The inside of the shaft of a long bone is filled with   8._____

   A.   yellow marrow   B.   compact bony cells
   C.   red blood cells   D.   gelatinous tissue

9.   Children's bones do not break so easily as those of older persons because their bones   9._____

   A.   are less flexible
   B.   do not carry so heavy a weight
   C.   contain more cartilage
   D.   receive better nutritional foods

10.   All of the following associations are correct EXCEPT: 10._____

   A.   Intracutaneous - within the layers of the skin
   B.   Hypodermic - beneath the skin
   C.   Subcutaneous - sweat glands over the entire skin surface
   D.   Diaphoresis - perceptible perspiration

11.   The PRIMARY purpose of melanin is to   11._____

   A.   provide variation in the toughness of the skin
   B.   prevent the more dangerous rays of the sun from damaging tissues
   C.   convert surface skin on certain parts of the body into horny material
   D.   dilate the blood vessels in the skin

12.   Of the following, the SAFEST treatment for corns on toes is to   12._____

   A.   apply a medicated moleskin plaster to the area
   B.   wear well-fitted shoes
   C.   cut off the mass of dead skin cells on the surface of the corn
   D.   apply a corn remover

13.   Of the following statements, the CORRECT one is: 13._____

   A.   Suntan preparations enable an individual to stay in the sun longer with less risk of burning than without their use.
   B.   Suntan lotions increase the speed of one's natural tanning mechanism.
   C.   Suntan preparations shut out burning ultraviolet rays.
   D.   The application of suntan preparations is more effective when used during exposure to direct mid-day hours of sun rather than used on hazy, lightly overcast days.

14.   To soften water,   14._____

   A.   calcium in a fluid state is added to the water supply
   B.   fluorides in small amounts are added to the water supply
   C.   sodium is substituted for the calcium and magnesium in the water
   D.   sodium is taken from the water supply by the addition of chlorine

15. All of the following are important in tooth development EXCEPT vitamin   15.____

    A. A   B. C   C. B   D. D

16. Of the following, the gland MOST closely related to muscular efficiency is the   16.____

    A. adrenal   B. gonads   C. pituitary   D. thyroid

17. The INCORRECT association of gland and location is: 17.____

    A. Pineal - brain cavity
    B. Parotid - below and in front of the ear
    C. Submaxillary - below each lower jaw
    D. Thymus - at the larynx

18. A urine analysis does NOT test for the   18.____

    A. possibility of diabetes
    B. presence of albumin
    C. evidence of bladder or kidney inflammation
    D. growth of polyps in the urinary tract

19. All of the following are basic taste sensations EXCEPT _____ sensations.   19.____

    A. hot and cold   B. sweet
    C. bitter   D. sour

20. The accumulation of an oxygen debt by a normally healthy individual engaged in sport activity is related MOST directly to   20.____

    A. lack of endurance
    B. limited residual air
    C. strenuous exercise
    D. failure of the hemoglobin to combine with oxygen

21. The CHIEF cause of heart disease in persons under 40 years of age is   21.____

    A. heredity   B. rheumatic fever
    C. obesity   D. elevated blood pressure

22. Binocular vision is MOST important in   22.____

    A. forming impressions of depth
    B. providing a clear image of item on which eyes are focused
    C. reducing strain in each of the eyes
    D. intensifying receipt of light rays on the retina

23. The INCORRECT association is: 23.____

    A. Cornea - transparent part of the outer layer of the eye
    B. Lens - part of the eye where light first enters to be focused on the retina
    C. Iris - muscle which controls the size of the pupil
    D. Sclera - hard protective outer layer of the eye

24. Of the following, the CORRECT statement is: 24.____

    A. Wearing eyeglasses will always make a person's eyes stronger.

B. If a person is able to see clearly, he can be sure he doesn't need glasses.
C. Glancing occasionally at some distant object when doing close work with the eyes helps prevent eye strain.
D. Wearing sunglasses gives the eyes complete protection from the sun.

25. All of the following are correct reasons as to why it is necessary to maintain good posture when reading a book EXCEPT: 25.____

A. Reading with the head bent forward strains the neck muscles
B. Viewing print at a sharp angle strains the eye muscles in their effort to focus
C. Studying a page in a book while lying down distorts the image on the page
D. Interpreting the printed page while sitting in a slouched position results in eye inflammation

26. In order to avoid eye fatigue during the viewing of a television program, the lighting arrangement in the room should provide light that   26.____

A. is reflected on the screen
B. brings about subdued general illumination of the room
C. provides sharp contrast between the television screen and the surrounding area
D. is located in the line of vision toward the screen

27. The SAFEST method of acquiring a suntan is the one in which   27.____

A. a preparation is applied to provide a protective covering during the exposure time
B. gradual exposure allows the skin to build natural resistance by increased pigmentation and thickening for an even tanning
C. exposure of the skin is started with reflected rays from water rather than from morning rays of direct sunlight
D. skin is exposed to noon-day rays

28. No amount of vitamin D will serve to promote normal bone development unless the diet includes, in adequate quantities,   28.____

A. calcium and phosphorus   B. sodium and sulfur
C. iron and magnesium   D. potassium and carbon

29. All of the following associations concerning milk are correct EXCEPT: 29.____

A. Pasteurization - destruction of the common pathogens found in milk
B. Homogenization - process of emulsifying milk
C. Irradiation - sterilization of raw milk
D. Centrifugalization - separation of cream from the milk

30. It is INCORRECT to state that cholesterol   30.____

A. metabolism is related to atherosclerosis
B. is a normal and essential constituent of human tissue
C. levels in the blood are related to intake of animal fats
D. levels in the blood are lowered by intake of saturated fats

31. Of the following, the one that is NOT an after-effect of rickets is   31.____

A. bow-legs   B. chicken breast
C. knock-knees   D. clubfoot

32. All of the following concerning amino acids are correct EXCEPT: 32._____

   A. All amino acids contain carbon, hydrogen, oxygen, and nitrogen
   B. Excess amino acids are stored in the involuntary musculature of the body
   C. Proteins are made up of amino acids
   D. Amino acids play an important role in maintaining both natural and acquired resistance to infection

33. Of the following, the CORRECT statement is: 33._____

   A. All people with rosy complexions are healthy
   B. Any food that does not smell or taste spoiled is safe to eat
   C. All children with heart murmurs will surely have heart trouble later on in life
   D. Most persons who look thin and underweight are not necessarily in poor health

34. In your health guidance period, you have a pupil with a long, thin trunk.   34._____
Classifying by somatotypes, you would list this pupil as a(n)

   A. mesomorph   B. endomorph   C. holomorph   D. ectomorph

35. All of the following associations are correct EXCEPT: 35._____

   A. Muscle cramp - sustained involuntary contractions
   B. Muscle twitch - minor irregular spasm
   C. Muscle spasticity - sustained tension
   D. Muscle hypertrophy - decreased size due to loss of elasticity

36. All of the following statements are correct EXCEPT: The   36._____

   A. mitral valve is between the left auricle and the left ventricle
   B. tricuspid valve is between the right auricle and the right ventricle
   C. aortic-semilunar valve is between the aorta and the right auricle
   D. pulmonary semilunar valve is between the right ventricle and the pulmonary artery

37. Urea is made in the   37._____

   A. kidneys   B. liver
   C. ureter   D. urinary bladder

38. Definite sensory centers in the brain have been found for all of the following EXCEPT   38._____

   A. hearing   B. pain   C. vision   D. equilibrium

39. Saliva is associated with all of the following glands EXCEPT the   39._____

   A. submaxillary   B. parotid
   C. fundic   D. sublingual

40. Plasma is more advantageous than whole blood in an emergency because it   40._____

   A. contains more white corpuscles
   B. does not have to be typed
   C. contains more red corpuscles
   D. contains more platelets

41. The last year was characterized by a decrease in all of the following EXCEPT   41.____

    A. poliomyelitis cases
    B. · tuberculosis deaths
    C. infant and maternal deaths from childbirth
    D. heart disease and blood vessel disturbances

42. All of the following associations are correct EXCEPT: 42.____

    A. Paul Burkholder - chloromycetin
    B. Philip Hench - cortisone
    C. Selman Waksman - streptomycin
    D. Benjamin Duggar - insulin

43. Tobacco has the effect of temporarily decreasing the appetite because it causes an   43.____
increased concentration of blood

    A. sugar   B. protein   C. salts   D. starches

44. The present state of research in the relationship between the incidence of lung cancer   44.____
and smoking indicates the presence of a definite relationship between lung cancer and

    A. cigarette smoking   B. pipe smoking
    C. cigar smoking   D. all of the above

45. If a pupil is overweight only because of food intake, the teacher can help guide him by all   45.____
of the following admonitions EXCEPT:

    A. *Gradually change your eating habits*
    B. *Eliminate your breakfast*
    C. *Be content to reduce slowly*
    D. *Practice self-control*

46. All of the following are enzymes of pancreatic juice EXCEPT   46.____

    A. amylopsin   B. ptyalin   C. steapsin   D. trypsin

47. A sprain in any part of the body PRIMARILY involves the _____ tissue.   47.____

    A. ligament   B. nerve   C. skin   D. muscle

48. A victim with a fractured neck should ALWAYS be transported lying on   48.____

    A. the stomach, face downward
    B. a stretcher
    C. his back, face upward
    D. a blanket

49. All of the following statements are correct EXCEPT   49.____

    A. In a fracture, crepitus is usually present, but in a dislocation there is no crepitus.
    B. In a fracture, deformity may vary in extent while in a dislocation, the deformity is
       usually marked.

C. In a dislocation, deformity recurs after the part is placed in its normal position, while in a fracture there is no deformity after the bone is placed in normal position.
D. In a dislocation, the head of the bone rotates with the rest of the bone, whereas in a fracture the bone moves as two bones or as a bone with a loose end.

50. All of the following are complete fractures EXCEPT a(n) _____ fracture.   50._____

   A. impacted   B. greenstick   C. Colles'   D. Pott's

KEY (CORRECT ANSWERS)

1. B	11. B	21. B	31. D	41. D
2. A	12. B	22. A	32. B	42. D
3. B	13. A	23. B	33. D	43. A
4. B	14. C	24. C	34. D	44. A
5. B	15. C	25. D	35. D	45. B
6. D	16. A	26. B	36. C	46. B
7. D	17. D	27. B	37. B	47. A
8. A	18. D	28. A	38. B	48. C
9. C	19. A	29. C	39. C	49. C
10. C	20. C	30. D	40. B	50. B

TEST 2

DIRECTIONS: Each question or incomplete statement is followed by several suggested answers or completions. Select the one that BEST answers the question or completes the statement. *PRINT THE LETTER OF THE CORRECT ANSWER IN THE SPACE AT THE RIGHT.*

1. The stimulant theobromine is found in all of the following EXCEPT   1.____

    A. cocoa   B. chocolate   C. tea   D. coffee

2. Recent research indicates that the appetite center or food intake control is located in the   2.____

    A. pancreatic gland
    B. hypothalamus located at the base of the brain
    C. nerve centers that are directly controlled by the big muscles
    D. duodenum

3. In general, all of the following act to reduce the vitamin content in any food EXCEPT   3.____

    A. storage at room temperature for long periods
    B. freezing
    C. excessive heat
    D. prolonged cooking

4. All of the following are vitamins EXCEPT   4.____

    A. thiamine   B. niacin   C. heparin   D. biotin

5. All of the following associations are correct EXCEPT: 5.____

    A. Antidermatitis - vitamin B_6
    B. Antihemorrhagic - vitamin K
    C. Antineuritic - vitamin B_1
    D. Antisterility - vitamin G

6. All of the following associations are correct EXCEPT: 6.____

    A. Sodium and potassium - normal beating of heart
    B. Iron and copper - making of hemoglobin
    C. Calcium and phosphorus - formation of bone
    D. Chlorine and sulphur - oxidative processes

7. Dry skim milk   7.____

    A. has the same butterfat content as homogenized milk
    B. contains considerably more fat and vitamin A than whole milk
    C. has butterfat removed
    D. loses a good deal of its nutritional value when stored for several months

8. A pupil should be referred for the pitch tone test if the FINAL score in the first audiometer   8.____
test screening shows a hearing loss of

    A. 1 to 5 decibels in both ears
    B. 6 to 9 decibels in one ear
    C. 12 or more decibels in one or both ears
    D. 9 decibels in both ears

9. MOST cases of deafness are caused by troubles in the   9.____

    A. outer ear   B. inner ear
    C. eustachian tube   D. middle ear

10. After a group of pupils has had the audiometer test and before another group of pupils   10.____
uses the ear phones, it is advisable for the teacher to

    A. cleanse the ear phones with alcohol and cotton
    B. dip the ear phones in a solution of peroxide and water
    C. continue the testing without touching the ear phones
    D. tell the next group of pupils to rub the ear phones with a handkerchief or piece of
        tissue

11. In MOST large cities, sewage is purified by   11.____

    A. aeration   B. chemical action
    C. exposure to sunlight   D. isolation

12. The use of hard water for bathing is less satisfactory than the use of soft water because   12.____
of all of the following reasons EXCEPT:

    A. Hard water contains more calcium and magnesium than soft water
    B. Hydrolysis is slower in hard water than in soft water
    C. The use of detergents made necessary by bathing in hard water produces a drying
        effect on the skin
    D. The additional use of soap and the more vigorous rubbing required by the use of
        hard water may irritate the skin

13. Research on the fluoridation of public water supplies at the recommended concentration   13.____
indicates that

    A. there is a significant difference in the general death rate between areas where fluo-
        ride is present and those where it is absent
    B. the amount of fluoride useful for the prevention of tooth decay is well below the
        toxic level
    C. the continued consumption of water treated with fluoride is harmful to adults suffer-
        ing from chronic illnesses
    D. the fluoridation of water has caused a comparatively high incidence of disfiguring
        mottled tooth enamel

14. The poisonous character of carbon monoxide is due to its tendency to unite chemically   14.____
with

    A. synovial fluid   B. cerebro-spinal fluid
    C. hemoglobin   D. gastric juice

15. With regard to a tourniquet, the one CORRECT first aid procedure, according to the   15.____
American Red Cross, is

    A. loosening it after 20 minutes
    B. having it released only by a physician
    C. placing it on the wound
    D. having it applied only by a physician or nurse

16. Of the following procedures for the periodic check-up of pupils' height and weight by the   16.____
health guidance teacher, the MOST desirable is the one in which the teacher

    A. judges the pupil's height and weight and records his (her) judgment as satisfactory
       or unsatisfactory on the pupil's health envelope
    B. asks the pupil whether he has increased in height and lost or gained any weight
       and records the answers on the pupil's health envelope
    C. measures but does not record the pupil's height and weight on the pupil's record
       since variations in these items indicate that height-weight charts are obsolete
    D. measures the pupil's height and weight and records the findings as a means of
       evaluating the cumulative record of growth of the pupil

17. In cases of lordosis, there is a marked tendency to assume a position of round shoulders   17.____
because in such cases,

    A. the body compensates for the backward shifting of the body weight
    B. too much weight is thrown on the forward edges of the lumbar vertebrae
    C. the erector spinal muscles in the thoracic region are shortened
    D. the pelvis tilts backward

18. All of the following associations of conditions and causes are correct EXCEPT: 18.____

    A. Carbuncle - infection of a sebaceous gland
    B. Wart - excessive growth of papillae of the skin
    C. Mole - overdevelopment of pigment cells under the epidermis
    D. Boil - infection, usually at the site of a hair follicle

19. All of the following associations are correct EXCEPT: 19.____

    A. Macula - point of clearest vision at the center of the retina
    B. Organ of corti - sense of hearing
    C. Tympanic membrane - sound vibrations
    D. Mastoid cells - body balance

20. All of the following associations are correct EXCEPT: 20.____

    A. Peristalsis - wavelike contractions that pass along a tube
    B. Catalysis - breaking down of body cells
    C. Catharsis - purgation
    D. Metastasis - transfer of disease from a primary focus to a distant one

21. A lesion in the cerebellum may cause   21.____

    A. aphasia   B. ataxia   C. atavism   D. asthenia

22. All of the following associations concerning inflammation are correct EXCEPT: 22.____

    A. Heat - calor   B. Redness - rubor
    C. Pain - dolor   D. Swelling - aden

23. When the term *febrile* is associated with a physical condition, it means that the condition   23.____
    is characterized by

    A. fibroids   B. weakness of an organ
    C. fever   D. decreased respiration

24. All of the following associations are correct EXCEPT: 24.____

    A. Hepatic - pertaining to the liver
    B. Herpetic - pertaining to hair
    C. Hemiplegic - pertaining to paralysis of one side of the body
    D. Hematic - pertaining to the blood

25. All of the following are important components of the visual act proper EXCEPT   25.____

    A. accommodation   B. interpretation
    C. convergence   D. fusion

26. Of the following, the LEAST desirable practice in viewing television is to   26.____

    A. have the room dark
    B. view the screen from directly in front
    C. have moderate indirect lighting of the room
    D. frequently shift the eyes away from the screen

27. Of the following, the INCORRECT association is: 27.____

    A. Sclera - white of the eye
    B. Cornea - window of the eye
    C. Lens - pupil of the eye
    D. Iris - shutter of the eye

28. If the length of the anteroposterior diameter of the eye is too great, the resulting condition   28.____
    is

    A. farsightedness   B. nearsightedness
    C. astigmatism   D. trachoma

29. When the health guidance teacher tests pupils' vision by means of the Snellen chart,   29.____
    he(she) is testing the pupils'

    A. near acuity   B. distance acuity
    C. depth perception   D. peripheral vision

30. All of the following statements concerning body temperature in normal, healthy persons   30.____
    are correct EXCEPT:

    A. During the 24-hour day, the highest temperature is registered in the late afternoon
        or early evening
    B. During the 24-hour day, the lowest temperature is registered between 2 and 4 A.
        M., provided the person is not working on a night job

C. The more or less rhythmic rise and fall of body temperature is not established until adolescence

D. In most normal people, the variations of temperature are so small that it is difficult to detect them without the use of a special thermometer

31. It has been found that, for most people, the BEST room temperature is about _____ °F with relative humidity of about _____.   31._____

A. 70; 50%   B. 65; 40%   C. 68; 68%   D. 75; 75%

32. The MOST accurate of the following tuberculin tests is the   32._____

A. Moro Test, using a tuberculin ointment
B. Von Pirquet Test, applying tuberculin to the scratched skin
C. Mantoux Test, injecting tuberculin preparation between the layers of the skin
D. Patch Test, applying tuberculin ointment to the skin by gauze and adhesive plaster

33. All of the following statements concerning tetanus are true EXCEPT: 33._____

A. Tetanus infection is likely only with puncture-type wounds
B. Barnyard soil probably has the highest incidence of tetanus infestation
C. Insignificant wounds often cause tetanus infection
D. Immediate cleansing of a wound is a prime step in avoiding tetanus

34. All of the following are symptoms of a simple fracture of a bone EXCEPT   34._____

A. deformity
B. swelling
C. a wound through the skin
D. tenderness of the area to touch

35. A student who appears in the playground with an infected wound should be barred from physical activities PRIMARILY because   35._____

A. other children may be infected
B. a scab may be ruptured
C. the spread of infection is likely
D. pain may result

36. Traumatic shock following injury is directly attributable to   36._____

A. pain
B. loss of blood through external or internal bleeding
C. psychological reactions
D. failure of enough blood to circulate

37. Of the following, the substance that is NOT commonly used as an emetic is   37._____

A. salt water   B. soap suds
C. baking soda   D. ammonia water

38. All of the following statements concerning heat exhaustion are correct EXCEPT: 38._____

A. In heat exhaustion, perspiration is usually profuse.
B. Unconsciousness resulting from heat exhaustion is rare.

40

C. Salt tablets help to prevent heat exhaustion.
D. Body temperature rises rapidly.

39. Of the following, the gland MOST closely related to muscular efficiency is the   39.____

    A. adrenal   B. thyroid   C. gonads   D. pituitary

40. A deficiency of vitamin A in the diet may result in a condition known as   40.____

    A. beri-beri   B. scoliosis
    C. night blindness   D. scurvy

41. The condition in which a student is unable to focus both eyes on an object at the same   41.____
time is termed

    A. strabismus   B. hyperopia
    C. emmetropia   D. scotoma

42. The *pressure point* MOST effective in controlling arterial bleeding of the forearm is   42.____
located

    A. near the wrist
    B. near the elbow
    C. on the outer surface of the upper arm halfway between the shoulder and the elbow
    D. behind the inner end of the collarbone

43. The time interval between the entrance of infectious germs into the body and the appear-   43.____
ance of the first symptoms is known as the _____ period.

    A. active   B. incubation   C. sequelae   D. prodromal

44. A condition which may result from a deficiency of vitamin C is known as   44.____

    A. beri-beri   B. rickets   C. scurvy   D. impetigo

45. Of the following, the contagious disease of the skin that the playground teacher should   45.____
recognize in order to protect others is

    A. conjunctivitis   B. lordosis
    C. Osgood Schlatter's disease   D. impetigo

46. Of the following, the symptom of heatstroke MOST frequently noted is   46.____

    A. an absence of perspiration
    B. mental confusion
    C. headache
    D. dilated pupils

47. A puncture wound is considered serious from the point of view that   47.____

    A. bleeding may be hard to stop
    B. injury to tissue may be extensive
    C. infection is likely to result
    D. multiple injury may result

48. Astigmatism is due PRIMARILY to

    A. a loss of elasticity in the lens
    B. the eyeballs' being too long
    C. an irregularity in the curvature of the eyeball
    D. an imbalance of eye muscles

48._____

49. With regard to respiration, it is CORRECT to state that

    A. in forced expiration, all of the air in the chest can be expelled
    B. the presence of carbon dioxide in the blood causes the brain area that controls breathing to act
    C. contraction of the muscles of the chest causes expiration
    D. every time one swallows, the windpipe is covered by the uvula

49._____

50. With regard to strains, all of the following are correct EXCEPT

    A. application of heat relieves the pain
    B. rubbing downward on the injured part aids the return flow of blood in the veins
    C. gentle massage helps loosen up the muscles
    D. rest is necessary

50._____

KEY (CORRECT ANSWERS)

1. D	11. B	21. B	31. A	41. A
2. B	12. B	22. D	32. C	42. D
3. B	13. B	23. C	33. A	43. B
4. C	14. C	24. B	34. C	44. C
5. D	15. B	25. B	35. C	45. D
6. D	16. D	26. A	36. D	46. A
7. C	17. A	27. C	37. D	47. C
8. C	18. A	28. B	38. D	48. C
9. D	19. D	29. B	39. A	49. B
10. A	20. B	30. C	40. C	50. B

TEST 3

DIRECTIONS: Each question or incomplete statement is followed by several suggested answers or completions. Select the one that BEST answers the question or completes the statement. *PRINT THE LETTER OF THE CORRECT ANSWER IN THE SPACE AT THE RIGHT.*

1. A short lapse of consciousness and a sudden momentary pause in conversation or movement is MOST suggestive of   1.____

   A. nephrosis   B. autism
   C. Friedreich's ataxia   D. petit mal seizure

2. Which one of the following diseases usually has a very poor prognosis?   2.____

   A. Hodgkin's disease   B. Slipped epiphysis
   C. Cerebral palsy   D. Eczema

3. Mononucleosis is an abnormal condition of the   3.____

   A. blood   B. liver   C. nerves   D. colon

4. Increased thirst, increased urination, loss of weight, and general fatigue are common symptoms of   4.____

   A. arthrogryposis   B. diabetes
   C. hepatitis   D. arthritis

5. Which one of the following is a disease of the ear?   5.____

   A. Ostitis   B. Otitis
   C. Omphalitis   D. Ophthalmia

6. Glomerulonephritis is a disease of the   6.____

   A. heart   B. stomach   C. kidney   D. larynx

7. Which one of the following is the disease that would MOST likely impair the ability to ambulate?   7.____

   A. Diabetes   B. Colitis
   C. Bronchiectasis   D. Spina bifida

8. The lay term *hunchback* is synonymous with   8.____

   A. kyphosis   B. scoliosis
   C. torticollis   D. spondylolisthesis

9. Which one of the following diseases involves a malformation of the heart?   9.____

   A. Hydrocele   B. Tetralogy of Fallot
   C. Myasthenia gravis   D. Lordosis

10. Of the following, the disease which would be included under the general classification *orthopedic* is   10.____

   A. lupus erythematosus   B. lymphedema
   C. Osgood-Schlatter's   D. opthalmospasm

11. Of the following cardiac classifications, the one the teacher would be LEAST likely to encounter is   11.____

    A. 4A   B. 3C   C. 4E   D. 2C

12. A fusion operation upon the spine is often undertaken to correct   12.____

    A. pelvimetry   B. paroxysm
    C. epiphysistis   D. scoliosis

13. The treatment program for slipped epiphysis is MOST similar to the program for   13.____

    A. torticollis   B. Perthe's disease
    C. polydactylism   D. nephrosis

14. Which one of the following is MOST likely to be associated with production of large quantities of mucous?   14.____

    A. Kyphosis   B. Bronchiectasis
    C. Lymphodenoma   D. Thyroid deficiency

15. Poor bladder control is MOST frequently associated with   15.____

    A. rheumatic fever   B. hemophilia
    C. club foot   D. torticollis

16. Which one of the following conditions is caused by the inflammation of the lower part of the intestine?   16.____

    A. Pyelitis   B. Transverse myelitis
    C. Regional ileitis   D. Hepatitis

17. In contrast with former treatment methods that called for intramuscular injections, oral medication is now frequently provided for treating   17.____

    A. diabetes   B. colitis   C. thyroiditis   D. myelitis

18. A cardiac child classified as 4E would be MOST apt to   18.____

    A. be placed in a health conservation class
    B. receive home instruction
    C. be placed in a regular class with limited physical activity
    D. be placed in a regular class following a short stay in a special class

19. An underweight child with a cardiac condition should be encouraged to   19.____

    A. add candy to his diet
    B. add carbohydrates such as bread and milk desserts to his diet
    C. maintain weight below normal since this insures a margin of safety should illness occur
    D. increase his intake of fluids and salt

20. When correctly used, the term *allergen* refers to   20.____

    A. a person who is allergic
    B. an antihistamine medication
    C. a substance which produces allergy
    D. the tendency to inherit an allergy

21. Which of the following is congenital?   21.____

    A. Meningitis   B. Gastroenteritis
    C. Chronic bronchitis .   D. Osteogenesis imperfecta

22. Spasm is a common characteristic of   22.____

    A. slipped epiphysis   B. otitis
    C. muscular dystrophy   D. asthma

23. A disease usually characterized by frequent vomiting and cramps is   23.____

    A. colitis   B. bronchitis
    C. myocarditis   D. empyemia

24. A lateral curvature of the spine is characteristic of   24.____

    A. scoliosis   B. lordosis   C. hypnosis   D. stenosis

25. Which of the following is one of the GREAT dangers of many forms of anemia?   25.____

    A. Brain deterioration   B. Secondary infection
    C. Mental deficiency   D. Bleeding

26. Arteriosclerosis is a disturbance of the _____ system.   26.____

    A. skeletal   B. endocrine
    C. nervous   D. circulatory

27. Of the following disorders, which one is NOT a form of cerebral palsy?   27.____

    A. Little's disease   B. Athetosis
    C. Mitral's stenosis   D. Spastic paralysis

28. The chin is rotated away from the side of the short, prominent muscle; the head is tilted   28.____
toward the affected side.
These symptoms are characteristic of

    A. talipes   B. torticollis
    C. ligamentitis   D. bursitis

29. A patient designated by a physician as *Class IID* is suffering from   29.____

    A. diabetes   B. polio
    C. tuberculosis   D. heart disease

30. A dorsal curvature is generally referred to as   30.____

    A. lordosis   B. kyphosis   C. scoliosis   D. curatosis

31. A disease that usually occurs in overweight boys and girls between the ages of ten and   31.____
thirteen years and is characterized by upper tibial epiphysitis is known as _____ disease.

    A. Pott's   B. Charcot-Tooth's
    C. Little's   D. Osgood-Schlatter's

32. A child whose walk is characterized by a scissors gait, with inward rotation and adduction of the legs, is probably suffering from   32.____

    A. Erb's palsy   B. spasticity
    C. osteogenesis imperfecta   D. spina bifida

33. Which of the following children will *generally* be placed in a regular class rather than in a health conservation class?   33.____

    A. Cardiopathic children
    B. Epileptic children
    C. Children with orthopedic handicaps
    D. Tuberculosis children

34. Which one of the following groups encompasses the LARGEST number of children? _____ children.   34.____

    A. Malnourished   B. Crippled
    C. Cardiac   D. Tuberculous

35. Rickets, a disease of nutrition manifested by disturbances in the general health and in the bones and joints, is caused by a lack of vitamin   35.____

    A. A   B. B   C. C   D. D

36. Rheumatic fever   36.____

    A. most often strikes children between the ages of nine and ten
    B. is generally thought to be a streptococcal infection
    C. is generally accompanied by pain in the region of the heart
    D. is contagious

37. A young girl in your health conservation class has to have a blood transfusion every two weeks.
She probably is suffering from   37.____

    A. gastritis   B. hepatitis
    C. nephritis   D. Cooley's disease

38. Differential diagnosis is MOST difficult in distinguishing between cases of   38.____

    A. poliomyelitis and meningitis
    B. aphasia and brain damage
    C. spasticity and athetosis
    D. leukemia and anemia

39. The MOST common complaint made by psychiatric patients is concerned with   39.____

    A. depression   B. panic   C. insomnia   D. fatigue

40. The one of the following which is MOST likely to cause the reappearance in old age of a previously compensated neurosis is   40.____

    A. decrease in social status, loss of persons and possessions or presence of injuries and illnesses
    B. decrease in sensory and cognitive capacities resulting in poor reality testing

C. cerebro-arteriosclerosis or other cerebrovascular disturbance
D. decrease in financial resources, resulting in heightened anxiety

41. Infectious mononucleosis is also known as 41.____

    A. Hodgkin's disease   B. glandular fever
    C. chorea   D. bronchiectasis

42. Which one of the following is non-inflammatory? 42.____

    A. Cystitis   B. Nephritis   C. Nephrosis   D. Pyelitis

43. Idiopathic epilepsy may be BEST characterized as a condition which 43.____

    A. is of unknown origin
    B. is a result of some trauma
    C. is not amenable to treatment
    D. may be safely ignored

44. Which one of the following conditions is characterized by loss of weight, sleeplessness, irritability, and bulging eyes? 44.____

    A. Tuberculosis   B. Overactive thyroid
    C. Myasthenia gravis D. Frederick's ataxia

45. Cardiac involvement may result from a previous acute, infectious disease. The disease referred to is 45.____

    A. streptococcus sore throat
    B. measles
    C. uremia
    D. enteric fever

46. A type of facial paralysis due to a neuritis of the facial nerve in the Fallopian canal is called 46.____

    A. Paget's disease   B. Bell's palsy
    C. endocarditis   D. encephalitis

47. A slipped epiphysis occurs MOST frequently in 47.____

    A. early adolescence   B. late adolescence
    C. pre-adolescence   D. early childhood

48. An electroencephalogram would NOT ordinarily be used in connection with 48.____

    A. epilepsy   B. ataxia   C. pyelitis   D. meningitis

49. Which of the following is characterized by lifeless muscle? 49.____

    A. Pott's disease   B. Flaccid paralysis
    C. Scoliosis   D. Colitis

50. Of the following diseases, the one that is NOT directly attributable to a specific vitamin deficiency is 50.____

    A. scurvy   B. beri-beri   C. tularemia   D. pellagra

KEY (CORRECT ANSWERS)

1.	D	11.	A	21.	D	31.	D	41.	B
2.	A	12.	D	22.	D	32.	B	42.	C
3.	A	13.	B	23.	A	33.	B	43.	A
4.	B	14.	C	24.	A	34.	A	44.	B
5.	B	15.	A	25.	B	35.	D	45.	A
6.	C	16.	C	26.	D	36.	B	46.	B
7.	D	17.	A	27.	C	37.	D	47.	A
8.	A	18.	B	28.	B	38.	B	48.	C
9.	B	19.	B	29.	D	39.	A	49.	B
10.	C	20.	C	30.	B	40.	A	50.	C

EXAMINATION SECTION

TEST 1

DIRECTIONS: Each question or incomplete statement is followed by several suggested answers or completions. Select the one that BEST answers the question or completes the statement. *PRINT THE LETTER OF THE CORRECT ANSWER IN THE SPACE AT THE RIGHT.*

1. The condition in which the coagulation time of the blood is prolonged is   1.____
    A. hematoma   B. hemolysis   C. hemoptysis   D. hemophilia

2. Of the following, the one LEAST associated with degeneration of blood   2.____
    vessels is
    A. arteriosclerosis   B. thrombosis
    C. atherosclerosis   D. homeostasis

3. Normally, the pulse rate is   3.____
    A. *higher* in children than in adults
    B. *lower* in women than in men
    C. *higher* when accompanied with low blood pressure
    D. *lower* when fever is present

4. Leucocytosis almost always indicates   4.____
    A. malnutrition   B. hemorrhage
    C. anemia   D. infection in the body

5. Prothrombin is formed in the   5.____
    A. bone marrow   B. liver   C. plasma   D. spleen

6. All of the following movements are possible in the cervical region of the   6.____
    spinal column EXCEPT
    A. lateral flexion   B. pronation
    C. hyperextension   D. rotation

7. All of the following associations of body joints are correct EXCEPT   7.____
    A. gliding – wrist   B. pivot – knee
    C. hinge – elbow   D. ball-and-socket - shoulder

8. If necessary, the whole process of digestion can take place chemically   8.____
    without the service of the
    A. stomach   B. liver
    C. small intestine   D. pancreas

9. Of the following, the one which is NOT absorbed by the body in the form in   9.____
    which it is consumed is
    A. fats   B. mineral salts   C. water   D. meat extracts

10. Cow's milk can be made more digestible by   10.____
    A. irradiation   B. homogenization
    C. pasteurization   D. refrigeration

11. Food allergy is brought about when an individual becomes sensitized to the   11.____
    A. combination of certain foods within the stomach
    B. eating of acid and starchy foods in a meal
    C. protein in a certain food
    D. intake of acids which enter the stomach and mix with the hydrochloric acid normally found in the stomach

12. Of the following associations of digestive fluid and enzyme activity, the   12.____
    INCORRECT one is:
    A. Intestinal juice – protein-splitting enzyme
    B. Saliva-starch – splitting enzyme
    C. Pancreatic juice – fat-splitting enzyme
    D. Gastric juice-sugar – splitting enzyme

13. The LARGEST source of body heat is the _____ system.   13.____
    A. nervous   B. digestive   C. tegumentary   D. muscular

14. The gland which plays the LEADING role in regulating the physiological   14.____
    processes of the body is the
    A. pituitary   B. adrenal   C. pancreas   D. thymus

15. All of the following concerning hyperthyroidism are correct EXCEPT that   15.____
    in this condition there is
    A. a tendency to gain weight
    B. an increase in the heart rate
    C. an enlargement of the thyroid gland
    D. protrusion of the eyeballs

16. The occurrence of epileptic seizures among school-age children is mostly   16.____
    of the type known as
    A. petit-mal   B. psychomotor   C. grand-mal   D. Jacksonian

17. It is INCORRECT to state that   17.____
    A. in many cases epileptic seizures can be controlled
    B. during an epileptic seizure, the individual is insensible to pain
    C. there is a high correlation between epilepsy and mental retardation
    D. predisposition to epilepsy may be discovered by recording the electric currents given off by the brain

18. The medulla oblongata contains all of the following centers EXCEPT the   18.____
    _____ center.
    A. cardiac   B. heat-regulating
    C. vasomotor   D. respiratory

19. The term *meninges* is associated LEAST with the   19.____
    A. callus   B. dura mater   C. pia mater   D. arachnoid

20. Of the following, the one MOST closely associated with cerebral palsy is   20.____
    A. spastic paralysis   B. encephalitis
    C. neuritis   D. meningitis

21. The use of specific drugs in treating ineffective diseases within the body is   21.____
classified as
    A. chemotherapy   B. gerontology
    C. immunology   D. stereochromy

22. It is INCORRECT to state that a toxoid   22.____
    A. is made from the poison produced by the germ of a specific disease
    B. is so treated that when injected into the bod it may cause discomfort but
       not the illness
    C. stimulates the body to develop its own antibodies
    D. brings about life-long immunization from a disease

23. Of the following, the one that represents artificial immunization against a   23.____
disease is
    A. recovering from an attack of whooping cough
    B. the result of exposure to streptococcal infections
    C. vaccination against smallpox
    D. the use of antibodies which prevent mononucleosis

24. All of the following are examples of antibodies EXCEPT   24.____
    A. precipitins   B. antitoxins   C. agglutinins   D. vaccines

25. All of the following associations of person and discovery are correct   25.____
EXCEPT
    A. Robert Koch – tuberculosis bacteria
    B. Gerhard Domagk – sulfanilamide
    C. Emil Behring – diphtheria toxin
    D. Alexander Fleming - streptomycin

KEY (CORRECT ANSWERS)

1.	D		11.	C
2.	D		12.	D
3.	A		13.	D
4.	D		14.	A
5.	B		15.	A
6.	B		16.	C
7.	B		17.	C
8.	A		18.	B
9.	A		19.	A
10.	B		20.	A

21.	A
22.	D
23.	C
24.	D
25.	D

TEST 2

DIRECTIONS: Each question or incomplete statement is followed by several suggested answers or completions. Select the one that BEST answers the question or completes the statement. *PRINT THE LETTER OF THE CORRECT ANSWER IN THE SPACE AT THE RIGHT.*

1. The vitamin MOST essential for the health of the gums is vitamin
   A. C   B. B   C. A   D. K

   1.____

2. Vitamin D and phosphorus are essential for the utilization of _____ in the body.
   A. iron   B. copper   C. iodine   D. calcium

   2.____

3. All of the following conditions are the result of a vitamin deficiency EXCEPT
   A. beriberi   B. pellagra   C. cretinism   D. rickets

   3.____

4. All of the following statements are correct EXCEPT:
   A. Iron is relatively high in foods of low moisture content.
   B. More than half of the iron in the body is in the hemoglobin of the red blood cells.
   C. Iron-deficient individuals can absorb more iron from food than healthy persons.
   D. When the diet's supply of iron is in excess of body needs, it is stored in the liver for later use.

   4.____

5. Of the following foods, the one with the LEAST number of calories is one
   A. cup of cooked spinach   B. medium raw orange
   C. cup of popped popcorn   D. cup of raw shredded cabbage

   5.____

6. Weight reduction is BEST realized if the individual
   A. consumes his daily allotment of foods but abstains from food every other day
   B. pursues a liquid diet until desirable weight is reached
   C. follows a diet including foods high in nutrients but low in calories
   D. routinizes daily exercise with a diet low in fats

   6.____

7. In bitter cold weather, regulation of the body temperature is accomplished MAINLY through the
   A. oxidation of organic foods
   B. activity of the muscles
   C. radiation from the surface of the sun
   D. increased respiratory action

   7.____

8. Of the following uses of water in the body, the INCORRECT one is that it
   A. makes enzyme action possible
   B. moistens the surfaces of the lungs for gas diffusion
   C. serves as a source of energy
   D. assists in hydrolytic changes during digestion

   8.____

9. If an individual takes a bitter medicine and swallows it quickly with water, he will experience more of the bitter taste if he first places it   9._____
   A. under the tongue   B. at the tip of his tongue
   C. to the side of the mouth   D. on the back of his tongue

10. Of the following body parts, the LONGEST is the   10._____
    A. trachea   B. meatus
    C. cecum   D. Eustachian tube

11. Physiologic radiation, conduction, and vaporization are MOST closely associated with the   11._____
    A. lungs   B. glands   C. kidneys   D. skin

12. The one NOT associated with the other three is   12._____
    A. enzyme   B. hormone   C. ketone   D. catalyst

13. All of the following terms are concerned with skin eruptions EXCEPT   13._____
    A. macules   B. ciliates   C. papules   D. vesicles

14. A chemical depilatory   14._____
    A. decreases the flow of perspiration to the body surface where it is applied
    B. removes hair permanently
    C. increases the rate of growth of hair
    D. causes the hair to become easily detached from the skin

15. In caring for the cuticle of the nails, the individual should NOT   15._____
    A. use hand lotions to keep the cuticle soft
    B. push the cuticle back from the end-edge of the nail
    C. cut off the cuticle when it starts to cover the nail
    D. direct the hangnail away from the cuticle before snipping it off

16. In regard to body temperature, the INCORRECT statement is: 16._____
    A. Mouth temperature recording is lower than that of the rectum.
    B. Since the heat-regulating center does not function well for a time after birth, new babies need to be kept somewhat warmer than adults.
    C. The body temperature record obtained in the armpit is higher than that obtained from the mouth.
    D. In the morning, body temperature is low because of relaxed muscles as well as lack of food.

17. A person who is in need of a dental bridge would MOST likely visit a   17._____
    A. pedodontist   B. periodontist   C. podologist   D. prosthodontist

18. Of the following types of teeth, the one that an individual is LEAST apt to find in the deciduous set is the   18._____
    A. bicuspid   B. cuspid
    C. lateral incisor   D. tricuspid

19. The end-organ receptors of the hearing process are located in the
    A. middle ear   B. cochlea
    C. semi-circular canals   D. Eustachian tube

19.____

20. In a school system, referral of a child for a class for the acoustically
handicapped is usually made when there is a hearing loss of
    A. five decibels in each ear
    B. ten decibels in either ear
    C. fourteen decibels in one ear
    D. twelve decibels or more in the better ear

20.____

21. The correction of a visual error by the use of a concave lens is MOST
closely associated with
    A. myopia   B. hyperopia   C. presbyopia   D. strabismus

21.____

22. Of the following associations, the INCORRECT one is:
    A. Exoporia – eye turned outward
    B. Emmetropia – normal vision
    C. Esophoria – myopic astigmatism
    D. Diplopia – perception of two images of a single object

22.____

23. With regard to LSD, the INCORRECT statement is:
    A. LSD is also known as lysergic acid diethylamide.
    B. LSD can be detected by its characteristic odor when taken on a lump of
       sugar.
    C. The term *bad trip* is associated with mental upsets caused by the use of
       LSD.
    D. LSD is derived from a fungus substance growing on plants.

23.____

24. Of the following, the one NOT classified as a hallucinogenic drug is
    A. methadone   B. marijuana   C. LSD   D. mescaline

24.____

25. All of the following are effects of cigarette smoking EXCEPT a(n)
    A. increase in the heart beat
    B. constriction of the coronary arteries
    C. increase in blood pressure
    D. rise in the metabolic rate

25.____

KEY (CORRECT ANSWERS)

1.	A		11.	D
2.	D		12.	C
3.	C		13.	B
4.	C		14.	D
5.	D		15.	C
6.	C		16.	C
7.	B		17.	D
8.	C		18.	A
9.	D		19.	B
10.	A		20.	D

21.	A
22.	C
23.	B
24.	A
25.	B

EXAMINATION SECTION
TEST 1

DIRECTIONS: Each question or incomplete statement is followed by several suggested answers or completions. Select the one that BEST answers the question or completes the statement. *PRINT THE LETTER OF THE CORRECT ANSWER IN THE SPACE AT THE RIGHT.*

1. A highly complex compound containing nitrogen essential for building and repairing of body cells and tissue is   1._____

    A. carbohydrates   B. fats   C. proteins
    D. vitamins   E. minerals

2. Which of these is *generally* considered superior to other sources of basic amino acids?   2._____

    A. Fats   B. Green leafy vegetables
    C. Poultry   D. Fruits
    E. Milk, eggs, and meat

3. The building stones for the manufacture of proteins in the body are   3._____

    A. amino acids   B. carbohydrates   C. fats
    D. thyroxin   E. bile

4. A *more highly* concentrated source of energy than either proteins or carbohydrates is   4._____

    A. hemoglobin   B. vitamins   C. sugars
    D. antibodies   E. fats

5. Two minerals related to the health of the bones are _____ and _____.   5._____

    A. calcium; phosphorous   B. copper; zinc
    C. chloride; iodine   D. fluorine; manganese
    E. sodium; iron

6. A condition in which the blood is deficient in either quality or quantity of red blood cells is   6._____

    A. arteriosclerosis   B. goiter
    C. schizophrenia   D. anemia
    E. myxedema

7. The CORRECT percentage of body weight of the adult in regard to water is   7._____

    A. 35%   B. 45%   C. 55%   D. 65%   E. 75%

8. The ability to do *better* physical labor may be achieved as a result of eating a breakfast containing both _____ and carbohydrates.   8._____

    A. vegetables   B. minerals   C. vitamins
    D. fats   E. fruits

9. The CHIEF reason for obesity is   9._____

    A. heredity   B. overeating
    C. glandular   D. psychological
    E. eating proteins only

10. The MOST effective method of determining sensitivity to food allergies is the _____ test.   10._____

    A. elimination   B. patch   C. skin
    D. Minnesota   E. Salmonellosis

11. The MOST sensible way to lose weight is to   11._____

    A. cut out breakfast
    B. cut out the noon meal
    C. cut out the evening meal
    D. discuss losing weight with your physician
    E. drink less water

12. Your activities are the products of the   12._____

    A. nervous system   B. endocrine system
    C. thyroid gland   D. parathyroid gland
    E. gonads

13. The products of the endocrine glands are called   13._____

    A. hormones   B. chromosomes   C. eugenics
    D. pneumococcus   E. toxins

14. Olfactory cells are important to us in regard to   14._____

    A. tasting   B. touching   C. hearing
    D. smelling   E. production

15. The taste buds are imbedded in the   15._____

    A. throat   B. tongue
    C. teeth   D. roof of the mouth
    E. esophagus

16. Excessive amounts of caffein may result in   16._____

    A. indigestion   B. nervousness   C. sleeplessness
    D. irritability   E. all of the above

17. On a camping trip, the BEST way to purify drinking water is to   17._____

    A. boil the water
    B. filter the water
    C. store the water in reservoirs and allow the impurities to settle
    D. chlorinate the water

18. Trichinosis is a disease which may result from eating insufficiently cooked   18._____

    A. veal   B. pork   C. mutton   D. fowl

19. The normal temperature of the human body is _____ degrees.   19._____

    A. 68   B. 90   C. 98.6   D. 99.4

20. The BEST treatment for a cold is to 　20.____

    A. take a laxative
    B. go to bed
    C. exercise vigorously to work up a sweat
    D. gargle

21. If sugar is found regularly in the urine, the disease which may be present is 　21.____

    A. diabetes   B. anthrax   C. rheumatism   D. beriberi

22. A psychiatrist specializes in the field of 　22.____

    A. psychology
    B. infectious diseases
    C. high blood pressure and other circulatory diseases
    D. mental or emotional problems

23. A person with persistent bad breath should 　23.____

    A. clean his teeth several times daily to kill the odor
    B. have a medical examination to determine the cause
    C. gargle several times daily to kill the odor
    D. chew gum when with other people

24. The BEST way for students to learn about health is by 　24.____

    A. listening to their family and friends
    B. personal experience
    C. a study of scientific facts
    D. listening to the radio

25. Sensitivity to proteins contained in pollen, feathers, etc. may be the cause of 　25.____

    A. tuberculosis   B. pyorrhea
    C. arthritis   D. hay fever

26. Identify the FALSE statement. 　26.____

    A. Ability to drive a car is directly related to maturity and judgment.
    B. It is safe for a good swimmer to swim alone in a regular swimming pool.
    C. A pedestrian should walk on the left side of the road so that he will face the cars coming from the opposite direction.
    D. Carrying a passenger on a bicycle is not a safe practice.

27. When a person who has been sick is recovering, he is said to be 　27.____

    A. regenerating   B. anemic
    C. convalescing   D. infectious

28. The tuberculin test is helpful in determining which 　28.____

    A. people are immune to tuberculosis
    B. people have been infected with tuberculosis germs and need to be x-rayed
    C. people have recovered from tuberculosis
    D. part of the body is infected

29. The disease MOST likely to be fatal is   29.____

    A. mumps   B. chicken pox
    C. scurvy   D. tetanus (lockjaw)

30. Identify the TRUE statement regarding the *killing of a fever* by drinking whiskey.   30.____

    A. There is neither harm nor value in this method.
    B. The use of whiskey to *kill a fever* is standard medical practice.
    C. It is a little-known method but one that is frequently of value.
    D. It is more dangerous than helpful.

31. The term *Basic 7* refers to the seven   31.____

    A. rules for saving the nutritive value of foods
    B. minerals required by the body
    C. food groups which we need daily
    D. vitamins found in food

32. Identify the MOST accurate statement about the effect of alcohol on muscular coordina-   32.____
tion.

    A. An alcoholic drink just before playing a round of golf will increase a player's muscu-
       lar coordination.
    B. The effect of alcohol on muscular coordination depends *largely* on the health of the
       individual.
    C. An alcoholic drink just before leaving a party will NOT decrease one's muscular
       coordination in driving an automobile.
    D. There is considerable evidence that the use of alcohol affects muscular coordina-
       tion.

33. If an artery in the lower forearm has been cut, the pressure should be applied   33.____

    A. between the cut and the wrist
    B. either at the wrist or the elbow
    C. between the cut and the elbow
    D. both at the wrist and the elbow

34. Which statement about posture is FALSE?   34.____

    A. Poor posture makes one appear less conspicuous.
    B. Carelessness is the cause of MOST poor posture.
    C. Poor posture increases fatigue.
    D. *Stand tall, Walk tall,* and *Sit tall* are the chief rules for good posture.

35. Beriberi, rickets, scurvy, and pellagra are _____ diseases.   35.____

    A. circulatory   B. nutritional
    C. communicable   D. occupational

36. Which statement about nutrition is FALSE?   36.____

    A. Most leafy vegetables are rich in vitamins and minerals.
    B. There is no harm in drinking orange juice and milk at the same meal.
    C. Fish is of no special value as a brain food.
    D. Drinking more than six glasses of water daily is fattening.

37. Another name for poliomyelitis is   37._____

    A. tonsilitis   B. goiter
    C. infantile paralysis   D. appendicitis

38. The mineral needed by red corpuscles in the blood to help them carry oxygen is   38._____

    A. iron   B. calcium   C. fluorine   D. phosphorus

39. Emotional instability in adults is MOST frequently attributed to   39._____

    A. heredity   B. heart conditions
    C. head injuries   D. childhood home life

40. Accidents due to _____ occur MOST often in the home.   40._____

    A. falls
    B. poisoning from drugs and cleansing materials
    C. burns and scalds
    D. gas poisoning

KEY (CORRECT ANSWERS)

1. C	11. D	21. A	31. C
2. E	12. A	22. D	32. D
3. A	13. A	23. B	33. C
4. E	14. D	24. C	34. A
5. A	15. B	25. D	35. B
6. D	16. E	26. B	36. D
7. D	17. A	27. C	37. C
8. D	18. B	28. B	38. A
9. B	19. C	29. D	39. D
10. C	20. B	30. D	40. A

TEST 2

DIRECTIONS: Each question or incomplete statement is followed by several suggested answers or completions. Select the one that BEST answers the question or completes the statement. *PRINT THE LETTER OF THE CORRECT ANSWER IN THE SPACE AT THE RIGHT.*

1.   Athlete's foot is caused by   1._____

     A.   streptococcus   B.   oxides   C.   bacillus
     D.   fungi   E.   streptomycin

2.   An adult has _____ permanent teeth.   2._____

     A.   26   B.   28   C.   30   D.   32   E.   36

3.   Although some digested foods are absorbed by the blood stream in the stomach, MOST   3._____
absorption takes place in the

     A.   liver   B.   pancreas
     C.   gall bladder   D.   large intestine
     E.   small intestine

4.   The LARGEST gland in the body is said to be the   4._____

     A.   liver   B.   brain   C.   heart
     D.   stomach   E.   large intestine

5.   Jaundice results from   5._____

     A.   excessive amounts of bile being produced
     B.   a shortage of lymph
     C.   bile ducts being blocked
     D.   an improper diet
     E.   none of the above

6.   When the feces is slowed down in its passage through the colon, a condition of _____   6._____
is the result.

     A.   diarrhea   B.   hemorrhoids   C.   indigestion
     D.   constipation   E.   jaundice

7.   Ulcers are *usually* caused by   7._____

     A.   irregularities in heart beat
     B.   varicose veins
     C.   rapid peristalic movement
     D.   excessive amounts of acid in the digestive juices
     E.   none of the above

8.   Sleeping pills *usually* contain   8._____

     A.   marijuana   B.   cocaine   C.   antitoxin
     D.   agglutinins   E.   hypnotics

9. The Schick test is administered to determine if a person is immune to   9.____

    A. diphtheria   B. scarlet fever   C. typhoid fever
    D. tuberculosis   E. none of the above

10. A vaccine is made up of   10.____

    A. botulism   B. trichinosis
    C. dead or weakened germs   D. anthrax
    E. brucellosis

11. Tuberculosis is caused by a   11.____

    A. virus   B. toxin   C. bacillus
    D. infection   E. toxoid

12. Hydrophobia is   12.____

    A. abnormal desire for water
    B. rabies
    C. abnormal fear of darkness
    D. drowning
    E. fear of heights

13. Poor posture among school-age children is a(n)   13.____

    A. orthopedic defect   B. poliomyelitis defect
    C. osteomyelitis defect   D. epidemiologist defect
    E. none of the above

14. _____ is(are) NOT used for the treatment of cancer.   14.____

    A. X-rays   B. Radium   C. Radioisotopes
    D. Hormones   E. Surgery

15. Hypochrondia describes a person who   15.____

    A. fears the dark   B. daydreams
    C. imagines illnesses   D. fears water
    E. enjoys burning things

16. Alcohol is *one* type of   16.____

    A. tranquilizer   B. pep pill   C. depressant
    D. stimulant   E. all of the above

17. Ophthalmology is a disease of the   17.____

    A. ears   B. nose   C. throat   D. eyes   E. feet

18. A basal metabolism test is taken to determine if   18.____

    A. the heartbeat is normal
    B. the thyroid gland is functioning properly
    C. constipation exists
    D. blood pressure is normal
    E. barbituates exist in the blood

19. The astigmatism test will determine the person's ability to   19.____

   A. see   B. hear   C. write   D. speak   E. reason

20. A skin specialist may also be called a   20.____

   A. chiropodist   B. epidemiologist   C. dermatologist
   D. podiatrist   E. none of the above

21. An electro-cardiograph   21.____

   A. photographs kidneys   B. charts heart beats
   C. records blood pressure   D. records reaction time
   E. photographs lungs

22. Regular vigorous physical exercise will gradually   22.____

   A. increase the number of body muscles
   B. develop good character traits
   C. develop a heart condition
   D. increase heart efficiency
   E. weaken a person

23. Another name for hernia is   23.____

   A. laceration   B. groin
   C. rupture   D. incision

24. The proceeds from the sale of a certain Christmas seal is used to fight   24.____

   A. cancer   B. heart diseases
   C. infantile paralysis   D. tuberculosis

25. The nutrient of _____ is acted upon by bacteria in the mouth to produce acids which   25.____
   dissolve tooth enamel.

   A. protein   B. ascorbic acid
   C. sugar   D. phosphorus

26. In the winter, many people place pans of water on the stove or radiator to keep the air in   26.____
   the house from becoming too dry.
   A MORE feasible and healthful way of keeping the air sufficiently moist is to

   A. keep the room temperature down to 68 or 70 degrees
   B. keep the temperature high - at least up to 80 degrees
   C. open the windows at least twice a day
   D. keep the air circulating with an electric fan

27. An approved first aid treatment would be to   27.____

   A. remove a foreign body from the ear with a matchstick
   B. use a tourniquet to stop bleeding from a minor wound
   C. give salt water and stimulants for heat exhaustion
   D. apply absorbent cotton directly to a burn or scald

28. A blood count of a person suspected of having appendicitis reveals that the number of white corpuscles is normal.
It may be concluded that the person

   A. probably has appendicitis
   B. probably does not have appendicitis
   C. is developing no resistance to fight a possible infection
   D. needs a blood transfusion

28.____

29. Artificial respiration is NOT applied for

   A. drowning   B. gas poisoning
   C. corrosive poisoning   D. electric shock

29.____

30. The term *enriched,* as applied by the government to bread, means bread made of white flour to which has been added

   A. milk, butter, or eggs
   B. iron and thiamine, niacin, and riboflavin
   C. protein, roughage, and fat
   D. calcium, vitamin C, and sugar

30.____

31. Fatigue due to sedentary or mental work is *usually* BEST relieved at the end of one's working hours by

   A. several cups of coffee
   B. eight hours of sleep
   C. a tepid shower
   D. recreational activity of a physical type

31.____

32. Which statement on alcohol and its uses is FALSE?

   A. Alcoholic beverages are useful in preventing and curing colds.
   B. Alcohol is to be avoided in the treatment of snake or spider bites.
   C. It is a mistake to take an alcoholic drink before going out in bitter cold weather.
   D. Alcohol has limited use as a medicine.

32.____

33. Normally, constipation is BEST avoided through the use of

   A. mineral oil
   B. yeast
   C. laxatives
   D. foods containing roughage

33.____

34. In attempting to eradicate tuberculosis, this disease should be considered *primarily* a(n)

   A. result of faulty nutrition
   B. infection
   C. emotional ailment
   D. hereditary disease

34.____

35. Gonorrhea is *frequently* a cause of

   A. stomach ulcers   B. insanity
   C. baldness   D. sterility

35.____

36. One purpose of a periodic health examination is the detection of all of the following diseases EXCEPT   36.____

    A. typhoid fever   B. heart disease
    C. cancer   D. high blood pressure

37. These hormones help to regulate various body functions. _____ is involved when we get excited or angry.   37.____

    A. Thyroxin   B. Adrenalin   C. Insulin   D. Pituitrin

38. To a person driving a car or riding a bicycle, peripheral vision is MOST useful for   38.____

    A. seeing better at night
    B. reading traffic signs more easily
    C. detecting moving objects at the sides
    D. judging more accurately the speed of approaching vehicles

39. Beer, wine, and whiskey should be considered   39.____

    A. foods   B. tonics
    C. stimulants   D. depressants

40. A good substitute for oranges as a source of vitamin C is   40.____

    A. tomatoes   B. beef
    C. cod liver oil   D. whole wheat bread

KEY (CORRECT ANSWERS)

1. D	11. C	21. B	31. D
2. D	12. B	22. D	32. A
3. E	13. A	23. C	33. D
4. D	14. D	24. D	34. B
5. C	15. C	25. C	35. D
6. D	16. C	26. A	36. A
7. D	17. D	27. C	37. B
8. E	18. B	28. B	38. C
9. A	19. A	29. C	39. D
10. C	20. C	30. B	40. A

TEST 3

DIRECTIONS: Each question or incomplete statement is followed by several suggested answers or completions. Select the one that BEST answers the question or completes the statement. *PRINT THE LETTER OF THE CORRECT ANSWER IN THE SPACE AT THE RIGHT.*

1. Digestion *actually* begins in the   1._____

   A. mouth   B. pharynx or throat
   C. trachea   D. stomach
   E. small intestine

2. Vomiting is *usually* an indication that there is also a disturbance in some part of the body   2._____
   other than the

   A. stomach   B. mouth   C. throat
   D. small intestine   E. large intestine

3. The normal breathing rate per minute for an adult is about   3._____

   A. 11 to 13   B. 14 to 16   C. 16 to 18
   D. 19 to 21   E. 21 to 23

4. The MOST important to life is   4._____

   A. milk   B. meat   C. vegetables
   D. water   E. fruits

5. Pneumonia causes an inflammation of the   5._____

   A. throat   B. lungs   C. stomach
   D. nose   E. kidneys

6. The circulatory system does NOT involve the body's   6._____

   A. blood   B. heart   C. lymphatic vessels
   D. spinal cord   E. blood vessels

7. To protect the body from infection and disease is the function of   7._____

   A. platelets   B. white blood cells
   C. red blood cells   D. hemoglobin
   E. gamma globulin

8. _____ carries blood away from the heart.   8._____

   A. Venules   B. Veins
   C. Arteries   D. Capillaries
   E. Descending vena cava

9. Defects that a person is born with are called   9._____

   A. endocarditis   B. congenital   C. cardiac
   D. rheumatic   E. mutations

10. The MOST complicated system in the body is the _____ system.   10._____

   A. circulatory   B. respiratory   C. nervous
   D. digestive   E. motor

11. The autonomic nervous system controls   11._____

    A. voluntary muscles   B. smooth muscle
    C. conditioned reflexes   D. sympathetic movements
    E. involuntary muscles

12. A *spastic* cannot control his   12._____

    A. nerves   B. muscles   C. emotions
    D. environment   E. thoughts

13. The colored portion of the eye is called the   13._____

    A. cornea   B. pupil   C. iris   D. sclera   E. retina

14. Your _____ is NOT one of your body's weapons against germs.   14._____

    A. skin   B. hairs   C. nose
    D. antibodies   E. phagocytes

15. Dizziness and faintness may be associated with a disturbance of the _____ system.   15._____

    A. nervous   B. respiratory   C. circulatory
    D. skeletal   E. none of the above

16. The LARGEST number of people are accidentally killed when   16._____

    A. swimming   B. driving   C. walking
    D. falling   E. flying

17. The LARGEST number of accidents occur   17._____

    A. at home   B. in the water
    C. on the playground   D. at airports
    E. on highways

18. Shock exists because of   18._____

    A. poor circulation of the blood
    B. rapid heart beat
    C. nervous tension
    D. drop in body temperature
    E. open wound

19. A floor burn would be considered a(n) _____ wound.   19._____

    A. incised   B. abrasion   C. laceration
    D. puncture   E. bruise

20. A doctor uses a sphygmomanometer to test   20._____

    A. reaction time
    B. heart beat
    C. pulse rate
    D. blood pressure
    E. amount of sugar in urine

21. Stuttering is *usually* due to
    A. emotional disturbance
    B. nervous tension
    C. high blood pressure
    D. lack of muscular control
    E. childhood diseases

21.____

22. The capacity of the lungs and heart to carry on their tasks during strenuous activity is called
    A. muscle endurance
    B. muscle tone
    C. cardiorespiratory endurance
    D. respiration

22.____

23. A chiropodist is a specialist who treats the

    A. eyes   B. ears   C. feet   D. nose   E. mouth

23.____

24. Malignant tumor is associated with
    A. tuberculosis   B. heart disease   C. rabies
    D. moles   E. cancer

24.____

25. The LARGEST pores of the body are found on the

    A. arms   B. legs   C. back   D. chest   E. feet

25.____

26. The chemical salt of _____, when found in drinking water or applied directly to the teeth, seems to help reduce tooth decay.

    A. chlorides   B. fluorides   C. sulphates   D. nitrates

26.____

27. When cold air or cold water hits the skin, the body reduces heat loss *principally* by
    A. expanding the pores in the skin
    B. generating more heat in the muscles
    C. reducing the size of the blood vessels in the skin
    D. making the heart beat faster

27.____

28. A cup of coffee with sugar but WITHOUT cream contains *only*
    A. vitamin B   B. calories
    C. protein   D. roughage

28.____

29. A deficiency of _____ is a cause of night blindness.

    A. iodine   B. protein   C. vitamin A   D. vitamin c

29.____

30. MOST authorities believe the usual cause of color blindness is that it
    A. is an inherited characteristic, and so runs in families
    B. may develop from looking at brightly colored lights, especially red ones
    C. is a contagious infection caused by a filterable virus
    D. is caused by an injury to the eyes

30.____

31. Active acquired immunity occurs when a person has a disease and then recovers from it. This is common for the diseases of _____ and _____.   31.____

    A. tuberculosis; malaria
    B. measles; chicken pox
    C. colds; pneumonia
    D. diabetes; anemia

32. It is TRUE that   32.____

    A. raw meat is of no special value in treating a black eye
    B. goiter may be cured by wearing a string of amber beads around the neck, if the beads are kept in constant contact with the enlarged thyroid gland
    C. snake oil will cure rheumatism if the oil is thoroughly rubbed into the affected parts
    D. men whose work is largely mental and who wear hats are more likely to become bald than other men

33. The condition of _____ frequently makes the air less healthful in the home, school, or office during the winter.   33.____

    A. dampness
    B. lack of sufficient oxygen
    C. too much carbon dioxide
    D. room temperature too high

34. Antitoxin pertains to   34.____

    A. immunization
    B. sterilization
    C. germ-killing drugs
    D. determination of susceptibility to a disease

35. When many people in a community have hookworm, it is *likely* that they   35.____

    A. eat poorly cooked pork
    B. go barefooted
    C. have an inadequate diet
    D. do NOT have the doors and windows of their homes screened

36. MOST people who are overweight are so because they   36.____

    A. exercise too little
    B. have inherited a tendency to be overweight
    C. have an underactive thyroid gland
    D. eat too much

37. A meal which consists of bread, macaroni, rice pudding, and cake contains an excess of   37.____

    A. protein
    B. vitamins
    C. carbohydrates
    D. fats

38. Which statement about sunburn is FALSE?   38.____

    A. Sunburn is similar to any other burn and should be treated in the same manner.
    B. If a person who is badly sunburned develops a fever, a doctor should be called.
    C. A severe sunburn may be more serious than other burns of like extent.
    D. There is no danger of getting sunburned on a cloudy day.

39. Goiter may be caused by a lack of _____ in the diet or drinking water.   39._____

    A. iodine   B. chlorine   C. fluorine   D. bromine

40. It is FALSE that   40._____

    A. secondary sex characteristics generally become evident at adolescence
    B. the female reproductive organs which produce eggs are called ovaries
    C. the male reproductive organs which produce sperm are called testes
    D. girls and boys mature on the average at the same age

KEY (CORRECT ANSWERS)

1.	A	11.	E	21.	A	31.	B
2.	A	12.	B	22.	C	32.	A
3.	C	13.	C	23.	C	33.	D
4.	D	14.	C	24.	E	34.	A
5.	B	15.	B	25.	C	35.	B
6.	D	16.	B	26.	B	36.	D
7.	B	17.	A	27.	C	37.	C
8.	C	18.	A	28.	B	38.	D
9.	B	19.	B	29.	C	39.	A
10.	C	20.	D	30.	A	40.	B

TEST 4

DIRECTIONS: Each question or incomplete statement is followed by several suggested answers or completions. Select the one that BEST answers the question or completes the statement. *PRINT THE LETTER OF THE CORRECT ANSWER IN THE SPACE AT THE RIGHT.*

1. A state health officer is *generally* a

   A. specialist
   B. physician
   C. health educator
   D. member of the bar association
   E. nurse

1.____

2. The SEVEREST forms of mental illnesses are classified as

   A. neurosis   B. psychosis
   C. sublimations   D. personality disorders
   E. peristalsis

2.____

3. Security is considered the number one need.
   It is BEST satisfied by

   A. achieving wealth
   B. attaining social position
   C. being wanted
   D. obtaining maximum physical health
   E. all of the above

3.____

4. The appendix

   A. aids in elimination   B. aids in respiration
   C. serves no function   D. fights bacteria
   E. aids in digestion

4.____

5. Diabetes is a disease of the

   A. pancreas   B. kidney   C. spleen
   D. gonads   E. veins

5.____

6. MOST all children are born

   A. with astigmatism   B. nearsighted
   C. farsighted   D. unable to hear
   E. blind

6.____

7. In these modern days, alcoholism is considered a

   A. habit   B. disease   C. sickness
   D. pleasure   E. weakness

7.____

8. Alcohol is absorbed directly from the

   A. small intestine   B. large intestine   C. stomach
   D. gall bladder   E. kidneys

8.____

9. Anesthetics produce   9.____

    A. a feeling of warmth   B. diseases
    C. a loss of pain   D. freedom from diseases
    E. tuberculosis

10. The PRIMARY fault of self-prescribed drugs is that they   10.____

    A. are too costly
    B. do not cure the cause
    C. are hard to get
    D. are too slow in acting
    E. weaken the taker

11. Disease-producing bacteria form a poison called   11.____

    A. pimples   B. toxins   C. inflammation
    D. spores   E. bacilli

12. _____ diseases last for a long period of time.   12.____

    A. Chronic   B. Cochlea   C. Anaesthetic
    D. Analgesic   E. Acute

13. Rocky Mountain spotted fever is spread by   13.____

    A. ants   B. dogs   C. feces   D. ticks   E. flies

14. Which word is NOT related to the others?   14.____

    A. Antitoxins   B. Antibodies   C. Phagocytes
    D. Vaccine   E. Intravenous

15. The MOST frequent cause of death is   15.____

    A. cancer   B. nephritis   C. tuberculosis
    D. heart disease E. skin disease

16. A group of similar cells working together is called a(n)   16.____

    A. organ   B. tissue   C. nucleus   D. nerve   E. bine

17. The contraction of striated muscle cells is controlled by the   17.____

    A. person   B. nerves   C. heart
    D. tissues   E. cartilages

18. The muscles are fastened to the bones at both ends by   18.____

    A. ligament   B. ossification   C. cartilages
    D. tendons   E. coccyx

19. The outer layer of the skin is called the   19.____

    A. callus   B. dermis   C. papillae
    D. epidermis   E. cuticle

20. Human eggs are produced in the

    A. vagina   B. uterus
    C. ovaries   D. fallopian tube
    E. conceptus

20.____

21. Heredity plays an important part in the transmission of

    A. cancer   B. color blindness   C. heart disease
    D. tuberculosis   E. streptococcus

21.____

22. Fatigue is produced by accumulations of dioxide and lactic acid in

    A. the muscle cells   B. lungs
    C. respiratory system   D. nerve cells
    E. cardiac muscles

22.____

23. _____ is NOT a function of the bones of the body.

    A. Support
    B. Attachment of muscles
    C. Manufacture of blood cells
    D. Protection
    E. Weight

23.____

24. A hernia, or rupture, is more common in

    A. young girls   B. middle-aged women
    C. infants   D. men
    E. older women

24.____

25. The mysterious crippling disease is known as

    A. muscular dystrophy   B. poliomyelitis
    C. tetanus   D. trichinosis
    E. cerebral palsy

25.____

26. An inflamed area containing pus is called

    A. blackhead   B. impetigo   C. pustule
    D. boil   E. fever blister

26.____

27. _____ is(are) the MOST important concerning vitamin D.

    A. Green vegetables   B. Lean meat
    C. Sunshine   D. Butter
    E. Fruits

27.____

28. To recover from tuberculosis, it is MOST important to

    A. rest a great deal
    B. move to a dry climate
    C. exercise by taking long walks
    D. take injections of tuberculin

28.____

29. The cooking of foods decreases their nutritional value in respect to

    A. proteins   B. starch   C. vitamins   D. fats

29.____

30. The _____ destroy disease germs by surrounding and devouring them.   30._____

    A. red corpuscles   B. white corpuscles
    C. blood platelets   D. interstitial cells

31. An unconscious person should be given _____ as a first aid measure.   31._____

    A. water   B. whiskey or brandy
    C. coffee or tea   D. nothing

32. The scientific name for the female reproductive cell is   32._____

    A. sperm   B. ovum   C. gamete   D. embryo

33. Little or no roughage is contained in   33._____

    A. raw fruits   B. whole-grain cereals
    C. sugar and candy   D. vegetables

34. The term *fracture,* as used in first aid, means a(n)   34._____

    A. bone out of joint   B. broken bone
    C. injury to a cartilage   D. severed tendon

35. A disease in which certain body cells seem to *grow wild,* thereby destroying the regular cells and tissues, is   35._____

    A. leprosy   B. ulcers   C. cancer   D. hernia

36. It is NOT advisable to use cathartics and laxatives regularly because they   36._____

    A. weaken the muscle tone of the intestines
    B. destroy the enzymes of digestion
    C. cause one to lose appetite
    D. cause one to lose weight

37. Diseases which can be transmitted from one person to another by germs are   37._____

    A. infectious   B. hereditary
    C. allergies   D. non-communicable

38. Where should a well on a hillside farmyard be drilled?   38._____

    A. At the bottom of the hill, if the barn, pigpen, and outdoor toilet are on the hill
    B. On the hillside above the farm buildings and stockyards
    C. At least 100 feet to the side of the farm buildings and stockyards
    D. The location is unimportant provided the well is completely covered at all times

39. The soft tissue which underlies the hard outer enamel of a tooth is called   39._____

    A. dentine   B. cement
    C. connective tissue   D. root

40. Which statement on the reliability and accuracy of health advertising over the radio is TRUE?   40._____

    A. It is very reliable since it is censored before being broadcast.
    B. It may be considered reliable since doctors often prescribe many of the health remedies advertised.

C. Most of it is reliable and can be believed by the public.
D. Much of it is of questionable reliability.

41. The *bends* is a(n)   41._____

   A. gymnastic movement
   B. disease of the intestinal tract
   C. disease of divers and caisson workers
   D. ailment due to inhaling dust

42. The BEST way for a right-handed person to arrange his chair and writing desk in a room   42._____
    with windows on one side *only* is so that _____ the windows.

   A. he will face
   B. his back will be toward
   C. his right side will be toward
   D. his left side will be toward

43. The blood test required by many states before a marriage license is issued is for the pur-   43._____
    pose of determining whether or NOT either party has

   A. hemophilia   B. tuberculosis
   C. gonorrhea   D. syphilis

44. _____ applies to the destruction of bacteria.   44._____

   A. Quarantine   B. Vaccination
   C. Disinfection   D. Inoculation

45. The age period in which lack of proper food results in the MOST harm is   45._____

   A. from birth to 6 years of age
   B. childhood (approximately 6-12 years)
   C. adolescence (approximately 12-18 years)
   D. early maturity (18-24 years)

———————

KEY (CORRECT ANSWERS)

1. C	11. B	21. B	31. D	41. C
2. B	12. A	22. A	32. B	42. D
3. C	13. D	23. E	33. C	43. D
4. C	14. E	24. D	34. B	44. C
5. A	15. D	25. A	35. C	45. A
6. C	16. B	26. C	36. A	
7. B	17. A	27. C	37. A	
8. C	18. D	28. A	38. B	
9. C	19. D	29. C	39. A	
10. B	20. C	30. B	40. D	

———————

EXAMINATION SECTION
TEST 1

DIRECTIONS: Each question or incomplete statement is followed by several suggested answers or completions. Select the one that BEST answers the question or completes the statement. *PRINT THE LETTER OF THE CORRECT ANSWER IN THE SPACE AT THE RIGHT.*

1. Dichloro-diphenyl-trichloroethane was used MOST effectively as a(n)   1._____

    A.   disinfectant   B.   termite preventative
    C.   moth preventative   D.   insecticide

2. Learning by constant repetition without being aware of the thought behind what is being   2._____
learned is

    A.   book learning   B.   automation
    C.   rationalization   D.   rote learning

3. To cure drug addiction, the A.M.A. believes that the BEST procedure is to   3._____

    A.   maintain stable dosages in addicts
    B.   furnish narcotics at no cost
    C.   establish withdrawal clinics
    D.   give constant control in a drug-free environment

4. The purpose of vaccines is to   4._____

    A.   reduce the causative organism
    B.   develop scar tissue
    C.   stimulate growth of antibodies
    D.   produce bacteriostasis

5. Of the following, the MOST dangerous of the narcotic poisons is   5._____

    A.   codeine   B.   opium   C.   heroin   D.   marijuana

6. If a teenage girl is careless about putting her clothes away,   6._____

    A.   put the clothing away for her
    B.   tolerate the situation
    C.   inspire her to be neat
    D.   lecture her

7. A two-year-old child that refuses to eat luncheon should   7._____

    A.   be forced to eat
    B.   be appeased
    C.   not be forced to eat, and the food should be removed without comment after a rea-
        sonable time has passed
    D.   be scolded

8. Thumbsucking should be eliminated by   8._____

    A.   satisfying the physical and emotional needs
    B.   mechanical restraints

    C. applying distasteful compounds
    D. punishment

9. During the first three years, the STRONGEST influence on the personality of a child is   9.____

    A. his friends
    B. the economic status of the family
    C. the social status of the family
    D. his relationships with his family

10. For twelve-year-old children, an allowance   10.____

    A. may be used as a training device
    B. should be provided
    C. encourages a distorted sense of values
    D. provides a means of disciplinary control

11. When a ten-year-old child temporarily becomes irritable and boisterous, the parents   11.____
should

    A. divert his attention   B. punish him
    C. cater to his whims   D. ascertain the reason

12. Parents should provide opportunities to habituate control of small muscles of the arms   12.____
when the child

    A. eats solid food
    B. makes an effort to feed himself
    C. eats in restaurants
    D. attends school

13. Concerning a six-year-old child, parents who insist on absolute perfection may   13.____

    A. hamper future accomplishments
    B. encourage good habits
    C. increase mutual love
    D. destroy imitative performance

14. Lefthandedness   14.____

    A. is an individual trait   B. should be corrected
    C. indicates a shortcoming   D. is a conditioned reflex

15. To reduce fears in children, parents should   15.____

    A. give affection   B. lecture them
    C. shield them   D. provide safeguards

16. When a new baby is expected, to encourage a sense of belonging, older children should   16.____
be allowed

    A. to anticipate another playmate
    B. no knowledge of the new baby
    C. to know, but not talk, about the new baby
    D. to share in the preparations

17. First aid care of a third degree burn requires 17.____

    A. oil and chalk mixture   B. sterile dressing
    C. antiseptic solution   D. healing ointment

18. Concerning teeth, 18.____

    A. dental caries appear most frequently between ages 12 and 20
    B. dental tartar should not be removed
    C. orthodontia is unimportant
    D. fluorides prevent all decay

19. Heat destroys bacteria by 19.____

    A. enucleation
    B. hemolysis
    C. coagulating protein
    D. making the cell wall permeable

20. The value of antihistaminic compounds lies PRIMARILY in their ability to 20.____

    A. increase intervals between infections
    B. relieve allergic manifestations
    C. immunize
    D. prevent the spread of infection

21. A test program which gives positive proof of drug addiction is through the use of 21.____

    A. hystidine   B. nalline
    C. chlorine   D. choline

22. Drug withdrawal symptoms in addicts are vomiting and changes in 22.____

    A. muscular control   B. nerves
    C. color of the skin   D. pupils of the eyes

23. The mother of a family should engage in social activities outside the home because they 23.____
will

    A. prepare her for earning a living should necessity arise
    B. help her to *grow* with her husband
    C. provide a means of solving the children's problems
    D. broaden her own viewpoints and continue development of her own personality

24. The BEST method of managing family finances is for the breadwinner to 24.____

    A. dole out the money when it is needed
    B. turn over all control to the spouse
    C. provide an allowance for each member of the family to use as he pleases
    D. plan cooperatively with the entire family

25. Non-conforming young children should be   25.____

    A. observed and trained while they are young
    B. permitted to outgrow their undesirable traits by themselves
    C. punished at rare intervals
    D. the subject of discussion between members of the family circle without others being present

26. The home can BEST benefit the mental health of its members through   26.____

    A. development of attitudes which result in appropriate emotional expression
    B. an elementary knowledge of psychiatry
    C. a check on the psychosomatics of the older members
    D. regular physical check-ups

27. When a child expresses fear of darkness on retiring, the BEST procedure is to   27.____

    A. make light of his fears
    B. compel him to accept the darkness
    C. provide a dim light
    D. shame him for his fears

28. Active immunity is acquired through   28.____

    A. production of antibodies
    B. imperviousness of skin tissue
    C. enzyme activity
    D. washing action of mucous membranes

29. To avoid detection, the heroin addict injects the   29.____

    A. nasal mucosa and the gums
    B. gums and the vagina
    C. nasal mucosa and the vagina
    D. conjunctiva

30. A highly dangerous and addictive synthetic narcotic is   30.____

    A. amidol   B. amidone   C. cobalamine   D. pyridoxine

————

KEY (CORRECT ANSWERS)

1.	D		16.	D
2.	D		17.	B
3.	D		18.	A
4.	C		19.	C
5.	C		20.	B
6.	C		21.	B
7.	C		22.	D
8.	A		23.	D
9.	D		24.	D
10.	A		25.	A
11.	D		26.	A
12.	B		27.	C
13.	A		28.	A
14.	A		29.	B
15.	A		30.	B

TEST 2

DIRECTIONS: Each question or incomplete statement is followed by several suggested answers or completions. Select the one that BEST answers the question or completes the statement. *PRINT THE LETTER OF THE CORRECT ANSWER IN THE SPACE AT THE RIGHT.*

1. Salk serum is administered to prevent 1.____

    A. measles   B. diphtheria
    C. poliomyelitis   D. whooping cough

2. Cancer of the blood is 2.____

    A. carcinoma   B. sarcoma   C. leukemia   D. epithelioma

3. The accepted treatment in severe and extensive radiation burns is to FIRST 3.____

    A. apply tannic acid generously
    B. apply wet sodium bicarbonate dressing
    C. bandage the burned area firmly
    D. put the patient to bed

4. A bed cradle is a device for supporting the 4.____

    A. back   B. knees
    C. bed covering   D. food tray

5. Pediculosis Capitus refers to 5.____

    A. baldness   B. athlete's foot
    C. lice   D. tics

6. The MAIN purpose of a good nursing chart is to 6.____

    A. aid the nurse's memory
    B. help the doctor in diagnosis and treatment
    C. prevent lawsuits
    D. protect the hospital

7. When an ice bag is applied, it should be 7.____

    A. kept filled with ice
    B. strapped in place
    C. removed every 15 or 20 minites
    D. removed every hour

8. Hepatitis is a disease of the 8.____

    A. renals   B. spleen   C. liver   D. pancreas

9. Bones are joined to one another with 9.____

    A. sinews   B. tendons   C. ligaments   D. membranes

10. Average adult pulse rate for a man is 10.____

    A. 64   B. 72   C. 80   D. 96

11. In MOST cases, to get a doctor in an emergency, call the   11.____

    A. nearest doctor   B. nearest hospital
    C. Red Cross   D. police emergency 911

12. Intravenous injections may be legally administered by the   12.____

    A. registered nurse   B. practical nurse
    C. nursing aide   D. home nurse

13. Persons who are likely to come in contact with communicable diseases are immunized by   13.____

    A. heredity   B. environment   C. asepsis   D. biotics

14. The temperature of water for a hot water bottle should NOT exceed   14.____

    A. 100° F   B. 150° F   C. 125° F   D. 175° F

15. The currently accepted treatment for arthritis is   15.____

    A. x-ray   B. cortisone
    C. aureomycin   D. gold injections

16. The MOST reliable temperature is that found in the   16.____

    A. rectum   B. axilla
    C. mouth   D. none of the above

17. An antiseptic solution recommended in first aid for slight skin scratches (abrasions) is   17.____

    A. concentrated boric acid
    B. tincture of merthiolate 1:1000
    C. iodine 2%
    D. tincture of green soap

18. The MOST frequent cause of death in the United States today is   18.____

    A. cancer   B. tuberculosis
    C. poliomyelitis D. heart ailments

19. Average adult temperature by rectum is _____°F.   19.____

    A. 99.6   B. 97.6   C. 98.6   D. 100.6

20. Metaplasia refers to disturbances of the   20.____

    A. mucous membranes B. epithelial tissues
    C. cartilage   D. basal metabolism

21. A subjective symptom is one that the patient   21.____

    A. feels   B. hears   C. sees   D. smells

22. A bed cradle   22.____

    A. keeps the patient's weight off the bed
    B. keeps the knees up
    C. elevates the feet
    D. keeps the weight of the covers off the patient

23. Statistics indicate that MOST youngsters start the drug habit with   23.____

    A. marijuana   B. heroin   C. cocaine   D. morphine

24. A *stroke* may be caused by   24.____

    A. cerebral hemorrhage   B. caecal dilation
    C. aortal thrombosis   D. pleural edema

25. The control of automatic breathing is located in the   25.____

    A. cerebrum   B. cerebellum
    C. spinal cord   D. medulla oblongata

26. The water for the baby's bath should be   26.____

    A. 90° F   B. 95° F   C. 100° F   D. 105° F

27. The Schick test indicates immunity to   27.____

    A. diphtheria   B. smallpox   C. tetanus   D. tuberculosis

28. Difficulty in speaking is known as   28.____

    A. asphyxia   B. aphasia   C. amnesia   D. anorexia

29. A *water blister* should be   29.____

    A. opened and drained
    B. left unbroken
    C. painted with iodine and bandaged
    D. soaked in hot epsom salt solution

30. The FIRST to be affected by the anesthetizing action of alcohol is the exercise of   30.____

    A. judgment   B. memory
    C. muscular coordination   D. control of speech

31. To the nervous system, alcohol acts as a   31.____

    A. depressant   B. stimulant   C. gratifier   D. agitator

32. Acute alcoholism may properly be labeled a psychosis because it involves   32.____

    A. intellectual limitations
    B. a loss of contact with reality
    C. emotional inadequacies
    D. bodily disease

33. *Cured* alcoholics   33.____

    A. can control the amount they drink
    B. cannot ever *drink normally*
    C. need moral help to drink within *normal limits*
    D. can drink some alcohol as long as they eat with it

34. Characteristic symptoms of chronic alcoholism include 34._____

    A. exiccosis   B. damage to brain tissue
    C. increase in weight   D. periods of depression

35. Alcohol is MOST often used excessively in order to 35._____

    A. induce sleep
    B. stimulate brain action
    C. overcome social inadequacy
    D. furnish temporary release from tensions

KEY (CORRECT ANSWERS)

1.	C	16.	A
2.	C	17.	C
3.	C	18.	D
4.	C	19.	C
5.	C	20.	C
6.	B	21.	A
7.	C	22.	D
8.	C	23.	A
9.	C	24.	A
10.	B	25.	D
11.	D	26.	C
12.	A	27.	A
13.	D	28.	B
14.	C	29.	B
15.	B	30.	A

31.	A
32.	B
33.	B
34.	D
35.	D

EXAMINATION SECTION
TEST 1

DIRECTIONS: Each question or incomplete statement is followed by several suggested answers or completions. Select the one that BEST answers the question or completes the statement. *PRINT THE LETTER OF THE CORRECT ANSWER IN THE SPACE AT THE RIGHT.*

1. The daily energy requirement in calories recommended by the National Academy of Sciences for the average high school girl is

   A. 1300 - 1500   B. 2400 - 2600
   C. 3000 - 3200   D. 4800 - 5000

   1.____

2. The recommended dietary protein allowance for an individual is LEAST influenced by the factor of

   A. sex   B. age
   C. type of activity D. weight

   2.____

3. Of the following, the substance which does NOT act as an emetic is

   A. mustard   B. ipecac
   C. sodium bicarbonate D. table salt

   3.____

4. Of the following diseases, the one which is NOT food-borne is

   A. diphtheria   B. pneumonia
   C. tuberculosis   D. scarlet fever

   4.____

5. Of the following, the disease which is caused by an agent in a different group from the agents causing the other three diseases is

   A. tobacco mosaic disease   B. typhus
   C. measles   D. polio

   5.____

6. Of the following, the one which is a highly contagious skin condition is ·

   A. eczema   B. hives
   C. impetigo   D. miliaria rubra

   6.____

7. Of the following, the antibiotic that has been found MOST effective in the treatment of tuberculosis is

   A. penicillin   B. aureomycin
   C. streptomycin   D. tetracycline

   7.____

8. Of the following, the animal used in standard practice for demonstrating vitamin C deficiency is the

   A. mouse   B. guinea pig
   C. rabbit   D. rat

   8.____

9. A drug that increases arterial pressure is known as a(n)

   A. vasoconstrictor   B. hemostat
   C. vasodilator   D. vesicant

   9.____

10. Drugs that contract or shrink tissues are known as   10.____

    A.   carminatives   B.   counterirritants
    C.   astringents   D.   analgesics

11. Toxic effects in children have resulted from the ingestion of excessive amounts of which   11.____
one of the following?

    A.   Vitamin A   B.   Vitamin B_{12}
    C.   Vitamin C   D.   Thiamine

12. The basal metabolism test is ordinarily used to indicate   12.____

    A.   hypertension
    B.   activity of the thymus gland
    C.   activity of the thyroid gland
    D.   rate of blood circulation

13. Of the following, the chemical MOST often chosen by dentists to produce general anes-   13.____
thesia is

    A.   chloroform   B.   nitrous oxide and oxygen
    C.   ether   D.   ethyl chloride

14. The branch of dentistry concerned with the treatment of gums and other tissues support-   14.____
ing teeth is

    A.   peridontia   B.   orthodontia
    C.   pedodontia   D.   prosthodontia

15. The material filling the root canal of a tooth is   15.____

    A.   dental pulp   B.   dentine
    C.   cementum   D.   enamel

16. When vitamin B_{12} is administered by mouth, it is of little or no value unless   16.____

    A.   it is part of the vitamin B complex
    B.   normal gastric juice is present
    C.   it has been extracted from liver
    D.   it is taken in capsule form

17. The *morale vitamin,* the lack of which may cause people to become depressed and irrita-   17.____
ble, is

    A.   ascorbic acid   B.   thiamine
    C.   riboflavin   D.   folic acid

18. The browning of cut fruits may BEST be slowed by   18.____

    A.   keeping them in a refrigerator
    B.   keeping them in water
    C.   treating them with lemon juice
    D.   sprinkling them with sugar

19. Eggs are sized according to which one of the following criteria?   19.____

    A. Average circumference of the eggs
    B. Average length of the eggs
    C. Weight of a dozen eggs
    D. Number of eggs to make one pound of dried egg powder

20. Another name for soft wheat flour is _____ flour.   20.____

    A. pastry   B. bread   C. enriched   D. gluten

21. The section of the hog in which trichinella worms MOST often encyst themselves is the   21.____

    A. liver   B. fat tissue
    C. brain   D. muscle tissue

22. A day or two after having been baked, some loaves of bread develop a ropy substance in   22.____
the center.
This rope is caused by

    A. excess of yeast in bread
    B. too rapid cooling of the bread
    C. mold
    D. bacteria

23. The *black and blue* area on the skin that results from a bruise is known medically as   23.____

    A. vitiligo   B. ecchymosis
    C. epithelioma   D. dystrophia

24. Of the following, the tissue that lines the hair follicle is called   24.____

    A. dermis   B. epidermis
    C. adipose   D. subcutaneous

25. Microscopic examination of the cross-section of hair shafts of people with straight hair   25.____
shows the hair shafts to be

    A. square   B. flat   C. round   D. oval

26. The outer layer of the hair shaft is called the   26.____

    A. cortex   B. medulla   C. cuticle   D. papilla

27. All of the following textile fibers are of plant origin EXCEPT   27.____

    A. cotton   B. flax   C. mohair   D. sisal

28. High quality fabric is produced from all of the follow-ing varieties of cotton EXCEPT   28.____

    A. Asiatic   B. Egyptian
    C. pima   D. Sea Island

29. The cocoon from which commercial silk fiber is obtained is spun by the larva of the moth   29.____

    A. Tinea pellionella   B. Bombyx mori
    C. Ceratomia catalpae   D. Carpocapsa pomonella

30. The HIGHEST grade of felt used in the manufacture of men's hats is made of a mixture   30.____
of

    A.   fur fibers including beaver
    B.   cotton kapok and wool
    C.   rabbit's hair and wool
    D.   cashmere alpaca and wool

31. The spices cinnamon and cassia are derived from   31.____

    A.   inner bark   B.   flower buds
    C.   seeds   D.   roots

32. Grain alcohol is converted into acetic acid by which one of the following processes?   32.____

    A.   Oxidation   B.   Reduction
    C.   Methylation   D.   Esterification

33. Calcium propionate (under various commercial names) is used in the baking industry to   33.____

    A.   activate the yeast
    B.   inhibit mold growth
    C.   reduce the quantity of baking powder ordinarily required
    D.   keep the bread soft

34. Invert sugar is a mixture of   34.____

    A.   lactose and glucose   B.   maltose and sucrose
    C.   fructose and glucose   D.   galactose and ribose

35. Dark spots occurring in canned foods are often caused by   35.____

    A.   reaction of tannin in the food and iron in the can
    B.   overcooking the food
    C.   oxidation of the tin coating of the can
    D.   use of hard water in canning

KEY (CORRECT ANSWERS)

1.	B		16.	B
2.	C		17.	A
3.	D		18.	C
4.	C		19.	C
5.	D		20.	D
6.	C		21.	D
7.	C		22.	A
8.	D		23.	B
9.	A		24.	B
10.	C		25.	C
11.	A		26.	D
12.	C		27.	C
13.	B		28.	D
14.	A		29.	C
15.	A		30.	A

31.	A
32.	C
33.	D
34.	C
35.	A

TEST 2

DIRECTIONS: Each question or incomplete statement is followed by several suggested answers or completions. Select the one that BEST answers the question or completes the statement. *PRINT THE LETTER OF THE CORRECT ANSWER IN THE SPACE AT THE RIGHT.*

1. The red color of preserved meats, such as corned beef, results from the addition to the pickling solution of   1.____

   A. sodium chloride   B. sodium nitrate
   C. sugar   D. vinegar

2. The enzyme bromelin, often used to tenderize meats, is derived from   2.____

   A. milk   B. cow's stomach
   C. pineapples   D. papaya plant

3. The gas ethylene is often used for   3.____

   A. ripening fruits
   B. manufacturing rayon
   C. fruit anesthetizing
   D. disinfecting air in sick rooms

4. Undercooked poultry may cause   4.____

   A. tularemia   B. brucellosis
   C. salmonella poisoning   D. trichinosis

5. Certain diseases must be reported to the Department of Health. Which one of the following is NOT required to be reported?   5.____

   A. Pneumonia
   B. Food poisoning occurring in a group of three or more cases
   C. Meningitis
   D. Trichinosis

6. Food charts indicate the amount of vitamin A in foods in terms of   6.____

   A. grams   B. International Units
   C. milligrams   D. micrograms

7. A #1 can is also called a 211 x 400 can because it   7.____

   A. is 211 mm in diameter and 400 mm high
   B. is 2 11/16" in diameter and 4" high
   C. is 211 mm in diameter and 400 cc in volume
   D. weighs 211 mg and is 400 mm high

8. In the proper cooking of the following foods, LOWEST temperature would be used for   8.____

   A. sauteeing onions   B. frying eggs
   C. scalding milk   D. broiling steak

9. All of the following are organic metabolites EXCEPT   9.____

   A. fat   B. glucose   C. protein   D. water

10. Accepting the broadest conventional definition of *life,* one would regard the simplest of organisms to be the

    A. amino acids   B. bacteria
    C. polypeptides   D. viruses

10.____

11. The common house fly belongs to the order

    A. Hymenoptera   B. Coleoptera
    C. Lepidoptera   D. Diptera

11.____

12. To which one of the following animal groups does Ascaris belong?

    A. Rotifers   B. Flatworms
    C. Segmented worms   D. Roundworms

12.____

13. Of the following organisms, the one which is autotrophic is

    A. Azobacter   B. Escherischia coli
    C. Nitrobacter   D. Lactobacilli

13.____

14. The ant-aphid relationship is an example of

    A. commensalism   B. mutualism
    C. parasitism   D. synergism

14.____

15. To tell when the sleeping subject is dreaming, experimental psychologists record

    A. dilation of the capillaries
    B. movements of the eyeball
    C. rate of respiration
    D. skin sensitivity to pain

15.____

16. A hormone which is secreted by the adrenal glands and which equips animals to prepare for emergencies is

    A. insulin   B. epinephrine
    C. thyroxin   D. progesterone

16.____

17. In humans, maintenance of constant body temperature is a prime function of the

    A. endocrines   B. skin
    C. muscles   D. excretory system

17.____

18. Henle's loop is part of the

    A. adrenal   B. vagus nerve
    C. nephron   D. optic chiasma

18.____

19. Which one of the following represents the BEST order of tissues in a woody stem, beginning with the outside?

    A. Xylem, phloem, cambium, pith
    B. Phloem, xylem, cambium, pith
    C. Xylem, cambium, phloem, pith
    D. Phloem, cambium, xylem, pith

19.____

20. The function of xylem tissue in the leaf is to _____ the leaf.   20._____

    A.   bring water to
    B.   transport water from
    C.   bring the chemical products of photosynthesis to
    D.   transport the products of photosynthesis from

21. The corn kernel or grain is classified as a(n)   21._____

    A.   seed   B.   fruit   C.   ovule   D.   ovary

22. At which one of the following sites does fertilization in humans USUALLY occur?   22._____

    A.   Fallopian tube   B.   Graafian follicle
    C.   Ovary   D.   Uterus

23. The pulse beat felt at the wrist is the immediate result of   23._____

    A.   systolic pressure
    B.   heart beat
    C.   venous response to heart beat
    D.   arterial pressure changes felt on the wall of the artery

24. Groups of traits that tend to be inherited as a unit are PROBABLY   24._____

    A.   multiple alleles   B.   closely linked
    C.   dominant   D.   sex-linked

25. Glycogen is stored in   25._____

    A.   bone and cartilage   B.   fatty tissue
    C.   liver and muscle   D.   small intestine

26. The ion that is ESSENTIAL for blood clotting is   26._____

    A.   iron   B.   copper   C.   calcium   D.   magnesium

27. A drug discovered in clover hay that is used to prevent blood clotting is   27._____

    A.   chloromycetin   B.   dicoumarin
    C.   digitalis   D.   meprobamate

28. To determine most easily whether a guinea pig is pure black or hybrid, the animal should   28._____
be mated with which one of the following types of guinea pigs?
A

    A.   pure black   B.   hybrid black
    C.   black of any type   D.   white

29. Colloidal particles CANNOT be removed from the dispersion medium by   29._____

    A.   ultrafiltration   B.   electrophoresis
    C.   dialysis   D.   sedimentation

30. Brownian movement may easily be demonstrated by having pupils view under the micro-   30._____
scope

    A.   protozoa   B.   a drop of oil
    C.   India ink   D.   tail of a goldfish

31. The theory of the inheritance of acquired characteristics was proposed by   31.____

     A.   Le Chatelier   B.   Lamarck
     C.   Pasteur   D.   Pascal

32. The polio virus USUALLY enters the body by way of the   32.____

     A.   nose   B.   mouth
     C.   wounds   D.   nervous system

33. Which one of the following tissues has the GREATEST amount of intercellular matrix?   33.____

     A.   Visceral muscle   B.   Connective tissue
     C.   Nerve tissue   D.   Epithelium

34. To determine the amount of protein in a food, the food is USUALLY analyzed for nitrogen   34.____
and the nitrogen content multiplied by

     A.   3.1   B.   6.25   C.   12.5   D.   25

35. The fundamental (population) unit of classification is the   35.____

     A.   species   B.   genus   C.   order   D.   phylum

KEY (CORRECT ANSWERS)

1.	B		16.	B
2.	C		17.	B
3.	B		18.	C
4.	C		19.	D
5.	A		20.	D
6.	B		21.	A
7.	C		22.	A
8.	B		23.	D
9.	D		24.	D
10.	D		25.	C
11.	D		26.	C
12.	D		27.	B
13.	A		28.	D
14.	B		29.	D
15.	B		30.	C

31.	B
32.	C
33.	B
34.	D
35.	A

TEST 3

DIRECTIONS: Each question or incomplete statement is followed by several suggested answers or completions. Select the one that BEST answers the question or completes the statement. *PRINT THE LETTER OF THE CORRECT ANSWER IN THE SPACE AT THE RIGHT.*

1. Of the following, the one alkaloid found in the seeds of the nux vomica plant is   1.____

    A. quinine   B. atropine
    C. morphine   D. strychnine

2. In the preparation of chlorine gas by the reaction of potassium permanganate and hydro-   2.____
chloric acid, the oxidation number of manganese changes from

    A. +4 to +2   B. +7 to +2   C. +2 to +7   D. +7 to 0

3. *We cannot know simultaneously with perfect accuracy both the position and velocity of a*   3.____
moving electron.
The above statement is known as the _____ Principle.

    A. Pauli Exclusion   B. Heisenberg Uncertainty
    C. Pauli Uncertainty   D. Heisenberg Exclusion

4. The hypothesis that matter has a dualistic nature, having both the properties of a wave   4.____
and the properties of particles was FIRST proposed by

    A. Max Planck   B. Albert Einstein
    C. Erwin Schrodinger   D. Louis de Broglie

5. The ionization constant of acetic acid is given by the expression   5.____

    A. $\dfrac{[H^+]}{[C_2H_3O_2^-]}$ B. $[H^+][C_2H_3O_2^-]$

    C. $\dfrac{[HC_2H_3O_2]}{[H^+][C_2H_3O_2^-]}$ D. $\dfrac{[H^+][C_2H_3O_2^-]}{[HC_2H_3O_2]}$

6. *If the conditions of a system initially at equilibrium are changed, the equilibrium will shift*   6.____
in such a way as to tend to restore the original conditions is a statement of

    A. Avogadro's Hypothesis   B. Le Chatelier's Principle
    C. Gibbs' Phase Rule   D. Gay-Lussac's Law

7. If a pure chemical compound is carefully analyzed and found to be made up of   7.____
                   29.1% sodium (atomic weight =23)
                   40.5% sulfur (atomic weight = 32)
                   30.4% oxygen (atomic weight = 16),
the simplest formula for the compound is

    A. Na_2SO_4 B. $Na_2S_2O_3$ C. Na_2SO_3 D. $Na_2S_4O_6$

8. In the reaction $2S_2O_3^= + I_2 \rightarrow S_4O_6^= + 2I$, which one of the following takes place?

    A. $S_2O_3 =$ is reduced
    B. $S_2O_3 =$ is oxidized
    C. I_2 is oxidized
    D. I_2 acts as a reducing agent

8.____

9. $2SO_2(g) + O_2(g) \rightleftarrows 2SO_3(g) + heat$
If in the above chemical equilibrium the concentration of SO_2 is doubled, there will be a(n)

    A. increase in the equilibrium constant
    B. increase in the rate constant
    C. change in the energy of activation
    D. shift in the equilibrium position

9.____

10. If a solution of copper (III) sulfate is electrolyzed between inert electrodes, for how many seconds must a current of 1.93 amperes flow to deposit 0.640g of copper metal?

    A. 965   B. 1000   C. 1930   D. 2000

10.____

11. Ammonia gas can be made by which one of the following processes?

    A. Contact   B. Haber   C. Ostwald   D. Hall

11.____

12. Bromine will form an addition compound when it is shaken with

    A. alcohol   B. carbon tetrachloride
    C. ethylene   D. methyl iodide

12.____

13. Assume that 0.300 gram atom weight of aluminum metal is combined with chlorine to form aluminum chloride.
Of the following, which one is CLOSEST to the number of grams of chlorine which are combined with the metal? (At. wt. Al = 27, Cl = 35.5)

    A. 0.900   B. 8.10   C. 32.0   D. 40.1

13.____

14. A by-product recovered from scouring of wool and used in cosmetic products is

    A. petrolatum   B. spermaceti
    C. paraffin wax   D. lanolin

14.____

15. Titanium dioxide is used in face powder PRINCIPALLY because it

    A. absorbs water without swelling
    B. makes powder adhere to the skin
    C. makes powder go on the skin smoothly
    D. has a powerful covering capacity

15.____

16. Quarternary ammonium compounds are used in beauty culture work to serve as

    A. germicides in sterilizing instruments
    B. bleaching agents
    C. ingredients in nail polish
    D. ingredients of face powder

16.____

17. Parahydroxybenzoic acid and its esters are used in cosmetics to act as which one of the following?

    A. Preservatives   B. Emulsifiers
    C. Plasticizers   D. Solvents

17.____

18. Which one of the following is a substance which is used as a solvent in nail polish?

18.____

  A.
```
   H
   |
  HC-C=O
   | |
   H OH
```
  B.
```
 H H H
 | | |
H-C-C-C-H
 | | |
 OH OH OH
```
  C.
```
   H
   |
  HC  -  C=O
   |     |
   H   H-C-H
         |
         H
```
  D.
```
 OH    OH
 |     |
 C  -  C
 ||    ||
 O     O
```

19. Nitro-cellulose is the CHIEF ingredient used in the manufacture of

    A. lipstick   B. liquid nail polish
    C. cleansing creams   D. hair tints

19.____

20. It is common practice in bleaching hair to speed up the action of the bleaching solution by adding which one of the following?

    A. NH_4OH B. $NaOH$ C. HCl D. H_2SO_4

20.____

21. When an egg is cooked, protein denaturation takes place because

    A. hydrogen bonds in the protein are broken
    B. condensation of amino acids takes place
    C. polypeptide bonds are broken
    D. polypeptide bonds are formed

21.____

22. Of the following, the one compound formed when bread is leavened by the action of yeast is

    A. C_2H_5OH B. $C_{12}H_{22}O_{11}$ C. $NaKC_4H_4O_6$ D. $NaHCO_3$

22.____

23. The ester added to foods to give a banana flavor is

    A. $HCOOC_2H_5$ B. $CH_3COOC_5H_{11}$
    C. $HOC_6H_4COOCH_3$ D. $CH_3(CH_2)_2COOC_2H_5$

23.____

24. Wheat flour generally has better baking qualities than other cereal flours because of its higher content of

    A. proteins   B. gluten   C. gliadin   D. fiber

24.____

25. Of the following, the reaction which takes place in developing a photographic negative is

25.____

    A. $2AgBr + Na_2S \rightarrow Ag_2S + 2NaBr$

    B. $3Ag + AuCl_3 \rightarrow 3AgCl + Au$

    C. $2AgBr + 3Na_2S_2O_3 \rightarrow 2NaBr + Na_4Ag_2(S_2O_3)_3$

    D. $2AgBr + C_6H_4(OH)_2 \rightarrow C_6H_4O_2 + 2HBr + 2Ag$

26. Sepia toning is accomplished in photography by using a toning solution, the active ingredient of which is   26.____

    A. $AuCl_3$ B. $K_3Fe(CN)_6$
    C. H_2PtCl_6 D. Na_2S

27. The one textile fiber among the following that looks like a flattened, twisted, opaque ribbon under the microscope is   27.____

    A.   wool   B.   silk   C.   rayon   D.   cotton

28. Of the following, the one substance used in the textile industry as a mordant, in preparing fireproof cotton cloth and in weighting silk, is   28.____

    A.   ammonium sulfate   B.   sodium stannate
    C.   Glauber's salt   D.   silicone

29. Both anions and cations are removed from tap water by passing the water through   29.____

    A.   manganese zeolite   B.   permutit
    C.   ion exchange resins   D.   silicates

30. Of the following, the one synthetic fiber made by the polymerization of acrylonitrile is   30.____

    A.   nylon   B.   dacron   C.   orlon   D.   rayon

31. Which one of the following bleaching agents should NOT be used on animal fibers?   31.____

    A.   Sodium hypochlorite   B.   Hydrogen peroxide
    C.   Sodium perborate   D.   Potassium permanganate

32. Which one of the following statements is NOT true?   32.____

    A.   Organic acids usually have a milder action on fabrics than do mineral acids.
    B.   Animal fibers are less resistant to acids than are vegetable fibers.
    C.   Animal fibers are more resistant to acids than are vegetable fibers.
    D.   Vegetable fibers are more resistant to alkalis than are animal fibers.

33. The type of dye which is applied by agitating a fabric in a bath of soluble reduced dye, and the subsequent exposure of the fabric to the air, is known as a _____ dye.   33.____

    A.   sulfur   B.   vat   C.   basic   D.   direct

34. An iron rust stain on cotton can BEST be removed by   34.____

    A.   treating it with soap solution
    B.   exposing it to sunlight
    C.   treating it with oxalic acid and then with ammonia
    D.   treating it with turpentine or benzine

35. Chlorine may be used safely to bleach   35.____

    A.   silk   B.   linen   C.   wool   D.   fur

KEY (CORRECT ANSWERS)

1.	D	16.	B
2.	C	17.	A
3.	B	18.	D
4.	D	19.	C
5.	D	20.	C
6.	B	21.	B
7.	C	22.	A
8.	D	23.	D
9.	D	24.	B
10.	A	25.	D
11.	B	26.	B
12.	C	27.	D
13.	C	28.	C
14.	D	29.	D
15.	D	30.	A

31.	D
32.	B
33.	B
34.	C
35.	B

TEST 4

DIRECTIONS: Each question or incomplete statement is followed by several suggested answers or completions. Select the one that BEST answers the question or completes the statement. *PRINT THE LETTER OF THE CORRECT ANSWER IN THE SPACE AT THE RIGHT.*

1. Of the following, the MOST important contribution of copper to a gold alloy used in dentistry is to increase the   1.____

    A.   tarnish resistance   B.   strength and hardness
    C.   melting point   D.   corrosion resistance

2. The hypnotic chloral hydrate is a derivative of   2.____

    A.   paraform   B.   ethanol
    C.   acetaldehyde   D.   chloric acid

3. The compound used MOST for fluoridation of water is   3.____

    A.   apatite   B.   cryolite
    C.   fluorspar   D.   sodium fluoride

4. Of the following substances, the one which is used as an anticoagulant for blood is   4.____

    A.   sodium citrate   B.   ammonium chloride
    C.   sodium salicylate   D.   arbutin

5. Of the following, the one radioactive isotope that is used in the diagnosis and treatment of thyroid disorders is   5.____

    A. U^{235} B. Co^{137} C. C^{14} D. I^{131}

6. Of the following, the one type of alcohol which upon oxidation will be changed first to its corresponding aldehyde and then to its corresponding acid is   6.____

    A.   primary   B.   secondary
    C.   tertiary   D.   quarternary

7. Of the following, the one important ingredient used in the preparation of most thermosetting plastics is   7.____

    A.   cellulose   B.   formaldehyde
    C.   phenol   D.   acetic acid

8. The degree of unsaturation of a fat or oil is determined by a test which yields which one of the following?
_____ number.   8.____

    A.   Baumé   B.   Reichert-Meissel
    C.   Saponification   D.   Iodine

9. Of the following, the group consisting of two water soluble vitamins is   9.____

    A.   A and B   B.   C and D   C.   B and C   D.   A and D

10. Assume that ammonium hydroxide is added to a cupric solution until a precipitate of $Cu(OH)_2$ is formed and the addition is continued until part of the precipitate has dissolved to give a deep blue solution.
If some ammonium chloride is then dissolved in the solution, which one of the following will occur?

    A.   The blue color will disappear.
    B.   More of the precipitate will dissolve.
    C.   More of the precipitate will settle out.
    D.   No change will take place.

10.____

11. Of the following, the one metallic sulfide that is separated from other metallic sulfides by an alkaline solution of sodium sulfide and sodium disulfide in qualitative analysis is

    A.   PbS   B.   HgS   C.   CuS   D.   CdS

11.____

12. The element essential for the utilization of iron in the synthesis of hemoglobin in the body is

    A.   magnesium   B.   iodine   C.   zinc   D.   copper

12.____

13. A refrigerating drug often used by dentists before incising an abscess is

    A.   ethyl alcohol   B.   ether
    C.   ethyl chloride   D.   carbon dioxide

13.____

14. Atoms that have the same atomic number but different atomic weights are called

    A.   isomers   B.   isomorphs   C.   isobars   D.   isotopes

14.____

15. If one ml of a saturated solution of AgCl contains 1×10^{-8} moles of Ag+, the solubility product of AgCl is 1 x

    A. 10^{-6} B. 10^{-10} C. 10^{-12} D. 10^{-16}

15.____

16. At 30° C, the solubility of Ag_2CO_3 ($K_{sp} = 8 \times 10^{-12}$) would be GREATEST in one liter of which one of the following?

    A.   0.10M $AgNO_3$ B.   0.10M Na_2CO_3
    C.   Pure water   D.   0.10M NH_3

16.____

17. $H_2C_2O_4 + KMnO_4 \rightarrow H_2O + CO_2 + MnO + KOH$
In the above reaction, what is the weight of 1 gram-equivalent of $H_2C_2O_4$ (M.W. = 90)?

    A.   18   B.   45   C.   90   D.   450

17.____

18. Which one of the following is NOT a direct product or a by-product of the Solvay process?

    A. NH_4NO_3 B. Na_2CO_3 C. $CaCl_2$ D. $NaHCO_3$

18.____

19. Of the following, the kind of radioactive emission NOT affected by an electromagnetic field is

    A.   alpha particles   B.   beta particles
    C.   gamma rays   D.   protons

19.____

20. Suppose a 2.0 mole sample of hydrazine (N_2H_2) loses 20 moles of electrons in being converted to a new compound X.
Assuming that all of the nitrogen appears in the new compound, what is the oxidation state of N in the new compound X?

    A.   -2   B.   +1   C.   +3   D.   +5

20.____

21. For the reaction $AB \rightleftarrows A + B + 80,000\,cal$, which one of the following is TRUE?

    A.   The value of K_{eq} changes with changes in temperature.
    B.   An increase in the concentration of B changes the value of $K_{eq.}$
    C.   The escape of B as a gas decreases the concentration of A, if AB and A are in solution.
    D.   An increase of temperature shifts the equilibrium point to the right, if all substances are gases.

21.____

22. The combustion of propane is given by the following equation:

$$C_3H_8(g) + 5O_2(g) \rightarrow 3CO_2(g) + 4H_2O(g).$$

The heat of formation of CO_2 is -94.0 kcal/mole.
The heat of formation of H_2O is -57.8 kcal/mole.
The heat of formation of $C_3H_8(g)$ is -24.8 kcal/mole.
The amount of heat produced by the combustion of one mole of propane, in kcal, is

    A. 127.0   B. 488.5   C. 513.4   D. 538.2

22.____

23. Of the following, the one that has the HIGHEST coefficient of cubic expansion at room temperature is

    A. ethanol   B. mercury   C. nitrogen   D. sodium

23.____

24. Of the following indicators, the one that is colorless in an acid solution is

    A. phenol red   B. methyl orange
    C. thymol blue   D. phenolphthalein

24.____

25. The organic acid commonly found in sour apples is

    A. malic   B. tartaric   C. citric   D. benzoic

25.____

26. Of the following, the statement that is TRUE concerning the compound X-O-H, where X is an element other than hydrogen, is that

    A. it must be a strong base
    B. a water solution of the compound cannot be an electrical conductor
    C. if X is very electronegative, the compound is an acid
    D. the oxidation state of the element O may have any value from -2 to +1

26.____

27. Which one of the following has the species arranged according to INCREASING boiling points?

    A. $NaBr, HBr, Br_2, H_2$ B. $H_2, Br_2, NaBr, HBr$
    C. $NaBr, HBr, H_2, Br_2$ D. $H_2, HBr, Br_2, NaBr$

27.____

28. Of the following, which BEST describes the bonds in silicon carbide?   28._____

    A.   Ionic   B.   Ion-dipole
    C.   Covalent   D.   Metallic

29. Which one of the following is a non-polar compound?   29._____

    A. CH_3Cl B. CH_2Cl_2 C. $CHCl_3$ D. CCl_4

30. Which one of the halogens given has the HIGHEST energy of hydration?   30._____

    A.   Fluorine   B.   Chlorine   C.   Bromine   D.   Iodine

31. The aldol condensation of acetaldehyde results in the formation of which one of the following?   31._____

    A. $CH_3CH_2OH + CH_3COOH$ B. $CH_3COCHOHCH_3$
    C. $CH_3CHOHCH_2CHO$ D. $HOCH_2CH_2CH_2COOH$

32. Which one of the following BEST describes the conversion of starch to glucose?   32._____

    A.   Oxidation   B.   Inversion
    C.   Hydrolysis   D.   Mutarotation

33. Conjugated double bonds are found in   33._____

    A.   propylene   B.   isoprene
    C.   allene   D.   butylene

34. Sublimation is a property generally associated with   34._____

    A.   lead   B.   silicon   C.   iron   D.   iodine

35. Which one of the following phase combinations CANNOT produce a colloid?   35._____

    A.   Solid in a solid   B.   Solid in a gas
    C.   Gas in a solid   D.   Gas in a gas

KEY (CORRECT ANSWERS)

1.	B		16.	C
2.	D		17.	D
3.	D		18.	A
4.	A		19.	C
5.	D		20.	D
6.	B		21.	A
7.	C		22.	D
8.	C		23.	C
9.	C		24.	D
10.	C		25.	A
11.	D		26.	A
12.	C		27.	B
13.	A		28.	C
14.	D		29.	D
15.	A		30.	A

31.	C
32.	C
33.	C
34.	D
35.	A

RECORD KEEPING
EXAMINATION SECTION
TEST 1

DIRECTIONS: Each question or incomplete statement is followed by several suggested answers or completions. Select the one that BEST answers the question or completes the statement. *PRINT THE LETTER OF THE CORRECT ANSWER IN THE SPACE AT THE RIGHT.*

Questions 1-15.

DIRECTIONS: Questions 1 through 15 are to be answered on the basis of the following list of company names below. Arrange a file alphabetically, word-by-word, disregarding punctuation, conjunctions, and apostrophes. Then answer the questions.

A Bee C Reading Materials
ABCO Parts
A Better Course for Test Preparation
AAA Auto Parts Co.
A-Z Auto Parts, Inc.
Aabar Books
Abbey, Joanne
Boman-Sylvan Law Firm
BMW Autowerks
C Q Service Company
Chappell-Murray, Inc.
E&E Life Insurance
Emcrisco
Gigi Arts
Gordon, Jon & Associates
SOS Plumbing
Schmidt, J.B. Co.

1. Which of these files should appear FIRST?   1.____

   A. ABCO Parts
   B. A Bee C Reading Materials
   C. A Better Course for Test Preparation
   D. AAA Auto Parts Co.

2. Which of these files should appear SECOND?   2.____

   A. A-Z Auto Parts, Inc.
   B. A Bee C Reading Materials
   C. A Better Course for Test Preparation
   D. AAA Auto Parts Co.

3. Which of these files should appear THIRD?   3.____

   A. ABCO Parts
   B. A Bee C Reading Materials
   C. Aabar Books
   D. AAA Auto Parts Co.

4. Which of these files should appear FOURTH?   4.____

    A. Aabar Books
    B. ABCO Parts
    C. Abbey, Joanne
    D. AAA Auto Parts Co.

5. Which of these files should appear LAST?   5.____

    A. Gordon, Jon & Associates
    B. Gigi Arts
    C. Schmidt, J.B. Co.
    D. SOS Plumbing

6. Which of these files should appear between A-Z Auto Parts, Inc. and Abbey, Joanne?   6.____

    A. A Bee C Reading Materials
    B. AAA Auto Parts Co.
    C. ABCO Parts
    D. A Better Course for Test Preparation

7. Which of these files should appear between ABCO Parts and Aabar Books?   7.____

    A. A Bee C Reading Materials
    B. Abbey, Joanne
    C. Aabar Books
    D. A-Z Auto Parts

8. Which of these files should appear between Abbey, Joanne and Boman-Sylvan Law Firm?   8.____

    A. A Better Course for Test Preparation
    B. BMW Autowerks
    C. Chappell-Murray, Inc.
    D. Aabar Books

9. Which of these files should appear between Abbey, Joanne and C Q Service?   9.____

    A. A-Z Auto Parts,Inc.   B. BMW Autowerks
    C. Choices A and B   D. Chappell-Murray, Inc.

10. Which of these files should appear between C Q Service Company and Emcrisco?   10.____

    A. Chappell-Murray, Inc.   B. E&E Life Insurance
    C. Gigi Arts   D. Choices A and B

11. Which of these files should NOT appear between C Q Service Company and E&E Life Insurance?   11.____

    A. Gordon, Jon & Associates
    B. Emcrisco
    C. Gigi Arts
    D. All of the above

12. Which of these files should appear between Chappell-Murray Inc., and Gigi Arts?   12.____

    A. CQ Service Inc. E&E Life Insurance, and Emcrisco
    B. Emcrisco, E&E Life Insurance, and Gordon, Jon & Associates
    C. E&E Life Insurance and Emcrisco
    D. Emcrisco and Gordon, Jon & Associates

13. Which of these files should appear between Gordon, Jon & Associates and SOS Plumb-   13.____
ing?

    A. Gigi Arts   B. Schmidt, J.B. Co.
    C. Choices A and B   D. None of the above

14. Each of the choices lists the four files in their proper alphabetical order except   14.____

    A. E&E Life Insurance; Gigi Arts; Gordon, Jon & Associates; SOS Plumbing
    B. E&E Life Insurance; Emcrisco; Gigi Arts; SOS Plumbing
    C. Emcrisco; Gordon, Jon & Associates; SOS Plumbing; Schmidt, J.B. Co.
    D. Emcrisco; Gigi Arts; Gordon, Jon & Associates; SOS Plumbing

15. Which of the choices lists the four files in their proper alphabetical order?   15.____

    A. Gigi Arts; Gordon, Jon & Associates; SOS Plumbing; Schmidt, J.B. Co.
    B. Gordon, Jon & Associates; Gigi Arts; Schmidt, J.B. Co.; SOS Plumbing
    C. Gordon, Jon & Associates; Gigi Arts; SOS Plumbing; Schmidt, J.B. Co.
    D. Gigi Arts; Gordon, Jon & Associates; Schmidt, J.B. Co.; SOS Plumbing

16. The alphabetical filing order of two businesses with identical names is determined by the   16.____

    A. length of time each business has been operating
    B. addresses of the businesses
    C. last name of the company president
    D. none of the above

17. In an alphabetical filing system, if a business name includes a number, it should be   17.____

    A. disregarded
    B. considered a number and placed at the end of an alphabetical section
    C. treated as though it were written in words and alphabetized accordingly
    D. considered a number and placed at the beginning of an alphabetical section

18. If a business name includes a contraction (such as *don't* or *it's*), how should that word be   18.____
treated in an alphabetical filing system?

    A. Divide the word into its separate parts and treat it as two words.
    B. Ignore the letters that come after the apostrophe.
    C. Ignore the word that contains the contraction.
    D. Ignore the apostrophe and consider all letters in the contraction.

19. In what order should the parts of an address be considered when using an alphabetical   19.____
filing system?

    A. City or town; state; street name; house or building number
    B. State; city or town; street name; house or building number
    C. House or building number; street name; city or town; state
    D. Street name; city or town; state

20. A business record should be cross-referenced when a(n)   20.____

    A. organization is known by an abbreviated name
    B. business has a name change because of a sale, incorporation, or other reason
    C. business is known by a *coined* or common name which differs from a dictionary spelling
    D. all of the above

21. A geographical filing system is MOST effective when   21.____

    A. location is more important than name
    B. many names or titles sound alike
    C. dealing with companies who have offices all over the world
    D. filing personal and business files

Questions 22-25.

DIRECTIONS: Questions 22 through 25 are to be answered on the basis of the list of items below, which are to be filed geographically. Organize the items geographically and then answer the questions.
    1. University Press at Berkeley, U.S.
    2. Maria Sanchez, Mexico City, Mexico
    3. Great Expectations Ltd. in London, England
    4. Justice League, Cape Town, South Africa, Africa
    5. Crown Pearls Ltd. in London, England
    6. Joseph Prasad in London, England

22. Which of the following arrangements of the items is composed according to the policy of: 22.____
Continent, Country, City, Firm or Individual Name?

    A. 5, 3, 4, 6, 2, 1   B. 4, 5, 3, 6, 2, 1
    C. 1, 4, 5, 3, 6, 2   D. 4, 5, 3, 6, 1, 2

23. Which of the following files is arranged according to the policy of: *Continent, Country,*   23.____
City, Firm or Individual Name?

    A. South Africa. Africa. Cape Town. Justice League
    B. Mexico. Mexico City, Maria Sanchez
    C. North America. United States. Berkeley. University Press
    D. England. Europe. London. Prasad, Joseph

24. Which of the following arrangements of the items is composed according to the policy of: 24.____
Country, City, Firm or Individual Name?

    A. 5, 6, 3, 2, 4, 1   B. 1, 5, 6, 3, 2, 4
    C. 6, 5, 3, 2, 4, 1   D. 5, 3, 6, 2, 4, 1

25. Which of the following files is arranged according to a policy of: *Country, City, Firm or*   25.____
Individual Name?

    A. England. London. Crown Pearls Ltd.
    B. North America. United States. Berkeley. University Press
    C. Africa. Cape Town. Justice League
    D. Mexico City. Mexico. Maria Sanchez

26. Under which of the following circumstances would a phonetic filing system be MOST effective?   26.____

    A. When the person in charge of filing can't spell very well
    B. With large files with names that sound alike
    C. With large files with names that are spelled alike
    D. All of the above

Questions 27-29.

DIRECTIONS: Questions 27 through 29 are to be answered on the basis of the following list of numerical files.

    1. 391-023-100
    2. 361-132-170
    3. 385-732-200
    4. 381-432-150
    5. 391-632-387
    6. 361-423-303
    7. 391-123-271

27. Which of the following arrangements of the files follows a consecutive-digit system?   27.____

    A. 2, 3, 4, 1   B. 1, 5, 7, 3
    C. 2, 4, 3, 1   D. 3, 1, 5, 7

28. Which of the following arrangements follows a terminal-digit system?   28.____

    A. 1, 7, 2, 4, 3   B. 2, 1, 4, 5, 7
    C. 7, 6, 5, 4, 3   D. 1, 4, 2, 3, 7

29. Which of the following lists follows a middle-digit system?   29.____

    A. 1, 7, 2, 6, 4, 5, 3   B. 1, 2, 7, 4, 6, 5, 3
    C. 7, 2, 1, 3, 5, 6, 4   D. 7, 1, 2, 4, 6, 5, 3

Questions 30-31.

DIRECTIONS: Questions 30 and 31 are to be answered on the basis of the following information.

    1. Reconfirm Laura Bates appointment with James Caldecort on December 12 at 9:30 A.M.
    2. Laurence Kinder contact Julia Lucas on August 3 and set up a meeting for week of September 23 at 4 P.M.
    3. John Lutz contact Larry Waverly on August 3 and set up appointment for September 23 at 9:30 A.M.
    4. Call for tickets for Gerry Stanton August 21 for New Jersey on September 23, flight 143 at 4:43 P.M.

30. A chronological file for the above information would be

    A. 4, 3, 2, 1   B. 3, 2, 4, 1
    C. 4, 2, 3, 1   D. 3, 1, 2, 4

30.____

31. Using the above information, a chronological file for the date of September 23 would be

    A. 2, 3, 4   B. 3, 1, 4   C. 3, 2, 4   D. 4, 3, 2

31.____

Questions 32-34.

DIRECTIONS: Questions 32 through 34 are to be answered on the basis of the following information.
1. Call Roger Epstein, Ashoke Naipaul, Jon Anderson, and Sarah Washington on April 19 at 1:00 P.M. to set up meeting with Alika D'Ornay for June 6 in New York.
2. Call Martin Ames before noon on April 19 to confirm afternoon meeting with Bob Greenwood on April 20th
3. Set up meeting room at noon for 2:30 P.M. meeting on April 19th;
4. Ashley Stanton contact Bob Greenwood at 9:00 A.M. on April 20 and set up meeting for June 6 at 8:30 A.M.
5. Carol Guiland contact Shelby Van Ness during afternoon of April 20 and set up meeting for June 6 at 10:00 A.M.
6. Call airline and reserve tickets on June 6 for Roger Epstein trip *to* Denver on July 8
7. Meeting at 2:30 P.M. on April 19th

32. A chronological file for all of the above information would be

    A. 2, 1, 3, 7, 5, 4, 6   B. 3, 7, 2, 1, 4, 5, 6
    C. 3, 7, 1, 2, 5, 4, 6   D. 2, 3, 1, 7, 4, 5, 6

32.____

33. A chronological file for the date of April 19th would be

    A. 2, 3, 7, 1   B. 2, 3, 1, 7
    C. 7, 1, 3, 2   D. 3, 7, 1, 2

33.____

34. Add the following information to the file, and then create a chronological file for April 20th:
    8. April 20: 3:00 P.M. meeting between Bob Greenwood and Martin Ames.

    A. 4, 5, 8   B. 4, 8, 5   C. 8, 5, 4   D. 5, 4, 8

34.____

35. The PRIMARY advantage of computer records filing over a manual system is

    A. speed of retrieval   B. accuracy
    C. cost   D. potential file loss

35.____

KEY (CORRECT ANSWERS)

1.	B		16.	B
2.	C		17.	C
3.	D		18.	D
4.	A		19.	A
5.	D		20.	D
6.	C		21.	A
7.	B		22.	B
8.	B		23.	C
9.	C		24.	D
10.	D		25.	A
11.	D		26.	B
12.	C		27.	C
13.	B		28.	D
14.	C		29.	A
15.	D		30.	B

31. C
32. D
33. B
34. A
35. A

INTERVIEWING

EXAMINATION SECTION
TEST 1

DIRECTIONS : Each question or incomplete statement is followed by several suggested answers or completions. Select the one that BEST answers the question or completes the statement. *PRINT THE LETTER OF THE CORRECT ANSWER IN THE SPACE AT THE RIGHT.*

1. Of the following, the MAIN advantage to the supervisor of using the indirect (or nondirective) interview, in which he asks only guiding questions and encourages the employee to do most of the talking, is that he can   1._____

    A. obtain a mass of information about the employee in a very short period of time
    B. easily get at facts which the employee wishes to conceal
    C. get answers which are not slanted or biased in order to win his favor
    D. effectively deal with an employee 's serious emotional problems

2. An interviewer under your supervision routinely closes his interview with a reassuring remark such as, "I'm sure you soon will be well," or "Everything will soon be all right." This practice is USUALLY considered   2._____

    A. *advisable,* chiefly because the interviewer may make the patient feel better
    B. *inadvisable,* chiefly because it may cause a patient who is seriously ill to doubt the worker's understanding of the situation
    C. *advisable,* chiefly because the patient becomes more receptive if further interviews are needed
    D. *inadvisable,* chiefly because the interviewer should usually not show that he is emotionally involved

3. An interviewer has just ushered out a client he has interviewed. As the interviewer is preparing to leave, the client mentions a fact that seems to contradict the information he has given.
    Of the following, it would be BEST for the interviewer at this time to   3._____

    A. make no response but write the fact down in his report and plan to come back another day
    B. point out to the client that he has contradicted himself and ask for an explanation
    C. ask the client to elaborate on the comment and attempt to find out further information about the fact
    D. disregard the comment since the client was probably exhausted and not thinking clearly

4. A client who is being interviewed insists on certain facts. The interviewer knows that these statements are incorrect. In regard to the rest of the client 's statements, the interviewer is MOST justified to   4._____

    A. disregard any information the client gives which cannot be verified
    B. try to discover other misstatements by confronting the client with the discrepancy
    C. consider everything else which the client has said as the truth unless proved otherwise
    D. ask the client to prove his statements

5. Immediately after the interviewer identifies himself to a client, she says in a hysterical   5.____
voice that he is not to be trusted.
Of the following, the BEST course of action for the interviewer to follow would be to

    A. tell the woman sternly that if she does not stay calm, he will leave
    B. assure the woman that there is no cause to worry
    C. ignore the woman until she becomes quiet
    D. ask the woman to explain her problem

6. Assume that you are an interviewer and that one of your interviewees has asked you for   6.____
advice on dealing with a personal problem.
Of the following, the BEST action for you to take is to

    A. tell him about a similar problem which you know worked out well
    B. advise him not to worry
    C. explain that the problem is quite a usual one and that the situation will be brighter
       soon
    D. give no opinion and change the subject when practicable

7. All of the following are, *generally,* good approaches for an interviewer to use in order to   7.____
improve his interviews EXCEPT

    A. developing a routine approach so that interviews can be standardized
    B. comparing his procedure with that of others engaged in similar work
    C. reviewing each interview critically, picking out one or two weak points to concen-
       trate on improving
    D. comparing his own more successful and less successful interviews

8. Assume that a supervisor suggests at a staff meeting that digital recorders be   8.____
provided for interviewers. Following are four arguments *against* the use of digital recorders
that are raised by other members of the staff that might be valid:
      I. Recorded interviews provide too much unnecessary information
      II. Recorded interviews provide no record of manner or gestures.
      III. Digital recorders are too cumbersome and difficult for the average
         supervisor to manage.
      IV. Digital recorders may inhibit the interviewee.
Which one of the following choices MOST accurately classifies the above into those
which are generally *valid* and those which are *not*?

    A. I and II are generally valid, but III and IV are not.
    B. IV is generally valid, but I, II and III are not.
    C. I, II and IV are generally valid, but III is not.
    D. I, II, III and IV are generally valid.

9. During an interview the PRIMARY advantage of the technique of using questions as   9.____
opposed to allowing the interviewee to talk freely is that questioning

    A. gives the interviewer greater control
    B. provides a more complete picture
    C. makes the interviewee more relaxed
    D. decreases the opportunity for exaggeration

10. Assume that, in conducting an interview, an interviewer takes into consideration the age, sex, education, and background of the subject.
This practice is GENERALLY considered   10._____

    A. *undesirable,* mainly because an interviewer may be prejudiced by such factors
    B. *desirable,* mainly because these are factors which might influence a person's response to certain questions
    C. *undesirable,* mainly because these factors rarely have any bearing on the matter being investigated
    D. *desirable,* mainly because certain categories of people answer certain questions in the same way

11. If a client should begin to tell his life story during an interview, the BEST course of action for an interviewer to take is to   11._____

    A. interrupt immediately and insist that they return to business
    B. listen attentively until the client finishes and then ask if they can return to the subject
    C. pretend to have other business and come back later to see the client
    D. interrupt politely at an appropriate point and direct the client's attention to the subject

12. An interviewer who is trying to discover the circumstances surrounding a client's accident would be MOST successful during an interview if he avoided questions which   12._____

    A. lead the client to discuss the matter in detail
    B. can easily be answered by either "yes" or "no"
    C. ask for specific information
    D. may be embarrassing or annoying to the client

13. A client being interviewed may develop an emotional reaction (positive or negative) toward the interviewer. The BEST attitude for the interviewer to take toward such feelings is that they are   13._____

    A. *inevitable;* they should be accepted but kept under control
    B. *unusual;* they should be treated impersonally
    C. *obstructive;* they should be resisted at all costs
    D. *abnormal;* they should be eliminated as soon as possible

14. Encouraging the client being interviewed to talk freely at first is a technique that is supported by all of the following reasons EXCEPT that it   14._____

    A. tends to counteract any preconceived ideas that the interviewer may have entertained about the client
    B. gives the interviewer a chance to learn the best method of approach to obtain additional information
    C. inhibits the client from looking to the interviewer for support and advice
    D. allows the client to reveal the answers to many questions before they are asked

15. Of the following, *generally,* the MOST effective way for an interviewer to assure full cooperation from the client he is interviewing is to   15._____

    A. sympathize with the client's problems and assure him of concern
    B. tell a few jokes before beginning to ask questions

C. convince the patient that the answers to the questions will help him as well as the interviewer
D. arrange the interview when the client feels best

16. Since many elderly people are bewildered and helpless when interviewed, special consideration should be given to them.
Of the following, the BEST way for an interviewer to *initially* approach elderly clients who express anxiety and fear is to

16.____

A. assure them that they have nothing to worry about
B. listen patiently and show interest in them
C. point out the specific course of action that is best for them
D. explain to them that many people have overcome much greater difficulties

17. Assume that, in planning an initial interview, an interviewer determines in advance what information is needed in order to fulfill the purpose of the interview.
Of the following, this procedure usually does NOT

17.____

A. reduce the number of additional interviews required
B. expedite the processing of the case
C. improve public opinion of the interviewer's agency
D. assure the cooperation of the person interviewed

17.____

18. Sometimes an interviewer deliberately introduces his own personal interests and opinions into an interview with a client.
In general, this practice should be considered

18.____

A. *desirable,* primarily because the relationship between client and interviewer becomes social rather than businesslike
B. *undesirable,* primarilv because the client might complain to his supervisor
C. *desirable;* primarily because the focus of attention is directed toward the client
D. *undesirable;* primarily because an argument between client and interviewer could result

19. The one of the following types of interviewees who presents the LEAST difficult problem to handle is the person who

19.____

A. answers with a great many qualifications
B. talks at length about unrelated subjects so that the interviewer cannot ask questions
C. has difficulty understanding the interviewer's vocabulary
D. breaks into the middle of sentences and completes them with a meaning of his own

20. A man being interviewed is entitled to Medicaid, but he refuses to sign up for it because he says he cannot accept any form of welfare.
Of the following, the *best* course of action for an interviewer to take FIRST is to

20.____

A. try to discover the reason for his feeling this way
B. tell him that he should be glad financial help is available
C. explain that others cannot help him if he will not help himself
D. suggest that he speak to someone who is already on Medicaid

21. Of the following, the outcome of an interview by an interviewer depends MOST heavily on the

    A. personality of the interviewee
    B. personality of the interviewer
    C. subject matter of the questions asked
    D. interaction between interviewer and interviewee

21.____

22. Some clients being interviewed by an interviewer are primarily interested in making a favorable impression. The interviewer should be aware of the fact that such clients are MORE likely than *other* clients to

    A. try to anticipate the answers the interviewer is looking for
    B. answer all questions openly and frankly
    C. try to assume the role of interviewer
    D. be anxious to get the interview over as quickly as possible

22.____

23. The type of interview which a hospital care interviewer usually conducts is *substantially different* from most interviewing situations in all of the following aspects EXCEPT the

    A. setting   B. kinds of clients
    C. techniques employed   D. kinds of problems

23.____

24. During an interview, an interviewer uses a "leading question."
This type of question is so-called because it, *generally.*,

    A. starts a series of questions about one topic
    B. suggests the answer which the interviewer wants
    C. forms the basis for a following "trick" question
    D. sets, at the beginning, the tone of the interview

24.____

25. An interviewer may face various difficulties when he tries to obtain information from a client.
Of the following, the difficulty which is EASIEST for the interviewer to *overcome* occurs when a client

    A. is unwilling to reveal the information
    B. misunderstands what information is needed
    C. does not have the information available to him
    D. is unable to coherently give the information requested

25.____

KEY (CORRECT ANSWERS)

1.	C	11.	D
2.	B	12.	B
3.	C	13.	A
4.	C	14.	C
5.	D	15.	C
6.	D	16.	B
7.	A	17.	D
8.	C	18.	D
9.	A	19.	C
10.	B	20.	A

21.	D
22.	A
23.	C
24.	B
25.	B

TEST 2

DIRECTIONS: Each question or incomplete statement is followed by several suggested answers or completions. Select the one that BEST answers the question or completes the statement. *PRINT THE LETTER OF THE CORRECT ANSWER IN THE SPACE AT THE RIGHT.*

1. Of the following, the MOST appropriate manner for an interviewer to assume during an interview with a client is

1.____

    A. authoritarian   B. paternal   C. casual   D. businesslike

2. The systematic study of interviewing theory, principles and techniques by an interviewer will, *usually*

2.____

    A. aid him to act in a depersonalized manner
    B. turn his interviewes into stereotyped affairs
    C. make the people he interviews feel manipulated
    D. give him a basis for critically examining his own practice

3. Compiling in advance a list of general questions to ask a client during an interview is a technique *usually* considered

3.____

    A. *desirable,* chiefly because reference to the list will help keep the interview focused on the important issues
    B. *undesirable,* chiefly because use of such a list will discourage the client from speaking freely
    C. *desirable,* chiefly because the list will serve as a record of what questions were asked
    D. *undesirable,* chiefly because use of such a list will make the interview too mechanical and impersonal

4. The one of the following which is usually of GREATEST importance in winning the cooperation of a person being interviewed while achieving the purpose of the interview is the interviewer's ability to

4.____

    A. gain the confidence of the person being interviewed
    B. stick to the subject of the interview
    C. handle a person who is obviously lying
    D. prevent the person being interviewed from withholding information

5. While interviewing clients, an interviewer should use the technique of interruption, beginning to speak when a client has temporarily paused at the end of a phrase or sentence, in order to

5.____

    A. limit the client's ability to voice his objections or complaints
    B. shorten, terminate or redirect a client's response
    C. assert authority when he feels that the client is too conceited
    D. demonstrate to the client that pauses in speech should be avoided

6. An interviewer might gain background information about a client by being aware of the person's speech during an interview.
Which one of the following patterns of speech would offer the LEAST accurate information about a client? The

6.____

A. number of slang expressions and the level of vocabulary
B. presence and degree of an accent
C. rate of speech and the audibility level
D. presence of a physical speech defect

7. Suppose that you are interviewing a distressed client who claims that he was just laid off   7.____
from his job and has no money to pay his rent.
Your FIRST action should be to

A. ask if he has sought other employment or has other sources of income
B. express your sympathy but explain that he must pay the rent on time
C. inquire about the reasons he was laid off from work
D. try to transfer him to a smaller apartment which he can afford

8. Suppose you have some background information on an applicant whom you are inter-   8.____
viewing. During the interview it appears that the applicant is giving you *false* information.
The BEST thing for you to do at that point is to

A. pretend that you are not aware of the written facts and let him continue
B. tell him what you already know and discuss the discrepancies with him
C. terminate the interview and make a note that the applicant is untrustworthy
D. tell him that, because he is making false statements, he will not be eligible for an
apartment

9. A Spanish-speaking applicant may want to bring his bilingual child with him to an inter-   9.____
view to act as an interpreter. Which of the following would be LEAST likely to affect the
value of an interview in which an applicant 's child has acted as interpreter?

A. It may make it undesirable to ask certain questions.
B. A child may do an inadequate job of interpretation.
C. A child 's answers may indicate his feelings toward his parents.
D. The applicant may not want to reveal all information in front of his child.

10. Assume you are assigned to interview applicants.   10.____
Of the following, which is the BEST attitude for you to take in dealing with applicants?

A. Assume they will enjoy being interviewed because they believe that you have the
power of decision
B. Expect that they have a history of anti-social behavior in the family, and probe
deeply into the social development of family members
C. Expect that they will try to control the interview, thus you should keep them on the
defensive
D. Assume that they will be polite and cooperative and attempt to secure the information you need in a business-like manner

11. If you are interviewing an applicant who is a minority group member in reference to his   11.____
eligibility, it would be BEST for you to use language that is

A. *informal,* using ethnic expressions known to the applicant
B. *technical,* using the expressions commonly used in the agency
C. *simple,* using words and phrases which laymen understand
D. *formal,* to remind the applicant that he is dealing with a government agency

12. When interviewing an applicant to determine his eligibility, it is MOST important to   12.____

    A. have a prior mental picture of the typical eligible applicant
    B. conduct the interview strictly according to a previously prepared script
    C. keep in mind the goal of the interview, which is to determine eligibility
    D. get an accurate and detailed account of the applicant 's life history

13. The practice of trying to imagine yourself in the applicant 's place during an interview is   13.____

    A. *good;* mainly because you will be able to evaluate his responses better
    B. *good;* mainly because it will enable you to treat him as a friend rather than as an applicant
    C. *poor;* mainly because it is important for the applicant to see you as an impartial person
    D. *poor;* mainly because it is too time-consuming to do this with each applicant

14. When dealing with clients from different ethnic backgrounds, you should be aware of certain tendencies toward prejudice.   14.____
Which of the following statements is LEAST likely to be valid?

    A. Whites prejudiced against blacks are more likely to be prejudiced against Hispanics than whites not prejudiced against blacks.
    B. The less a white is in competition with blacks, the less likely he is to be prejudiced against them.
    C. Persons who have moved from one social group to another are likely to retain the attitudes and prejudices of their original social group.
    D. When there are few blacks or Hispanics in a project, whites are less likely to be prejudiced against them than when there are many.

15. Of the following, the one who is MOST likely to be a good interviewer of people seeking assistance, is one who   15.____

    A. tries to get applicants to apply to another agency instead
    B. believes that it is necessary to get as much pertinent information as possible in order to determine the applicant's real needs
    C. believes that people who seek assistance are likely to have persons with a history of irresponsible behavior in their households
    D. is convinced that there is no need for a request for assistance

KEYS (CORRECT ANSWERS)

1.	D		6.	C
2.	D		7.	A
3.	A		8.	B
4.	A		9.	C
5.	B		10.	D

11.	C
12.	C
13.	A
14.	C
15.	B

———

GLOSSARY OF MEDICAL TERMS

CONTENTS

GLOSSARY OF MEDICAL TERMS

A

Abduction
Movement of limb away from middle line of the body.

Abrasion
A scraping away of a portion of the skin.

Abscess
Localized collection of pus or matter.

Acetabulum
Cup-shaped depression on external surface of the pelvic bone (innominate) into which the head of femur, or thighbone, fits.

Achilles Reflex
Movement of foot downward when the tendon immediately above the heel bone is struck.

Acromion
Process of bone constituting tip of shoulder.

Adduction
Movement of limb toward middle line of body.

Adhesion
The matting together of two surfaces by inflammation.

Alae Nash
Outer flaring walls of the nostrils.

Allergic
Reaction of tissues of the body to a protein substance to which the body is especially sensitive.

Anemia
A condition in which the red blood cells and/or hemoglobin are reduced.

Aneurysm
Sac, filled with blood, formed by the local dilation of walls of artery.

Angina Pectoris
Pain in chest associated with heart disease.

Ankyloses
Complete absence of motion at a joint.

Anterior
The anatomical "front" of the body.

Aorta
Main trunk of the systemic arterial system, arising from base of left ventricle.

Apex
Extremity of conical or pyramidal structure, such as heart or lung.

Aphasia
Loss of power of speech by damage to speech center.

Apoplexy
Another word for stroke.

Arrhythmia
Loss of normal rhythm of the heart.

Arteriosclerosis
Hardening of the arteries.

Artery

Blood vessel conveying blood away from the heart to different parts of the body.

Arthritis

Inflammation of a joint.

Arthrodesis

Stiffening of a joint.

Articulation

Joint.

Asbestosis

Dust disease of asbestos workers.

Aseptic

Free of germs.

Aspiration

Withdrawal, by suction, of air or fluid from any cavity.

Asthma

Disease marked by recurrent attacks of shortness, of breath, due to temporary change in bronchial tubes, making person uncomfortable.

Astigmatism

An abnormality in the curve of the 'anterior visual surface of the eyeball.

Astragalus

One of the ankle bones.

Ataxia

Disturbance of coordination of muscular movements.

Atelectasis

Collapse of lung tissue due to failure of entrance of air into air-cells.

Atrophy

Wasting or diminution in size of a structure.

Audiogram

Graphic record made by an audiometer, an electrical instrument for recording acuity of hearing.

Auricular fibrillation

Irregular beat as to time and force beginning in auricle of the heart.

Auscultation

The act of listening to sounds within the body.

Axillary

Relating to armpit.

B

Baker's Cyst

Enlargement of synovial sac in the back of the knee joint.

Basal Metabolism

The energy expended for the absolute minimum requirements of the body at complete rest.

Bell's Palsy

A form of facial paralysis.

Benign

Not malignant.

Biceps Muscle

A muscle over front of arm.

Bifida
Split or cleft.
Bilateral
Relating to or having two sides.
Blood Pressure
Pressure or tension of the blood within the arteries.
Brachial
Pertaining to the arm.
Bradycardia
Abnormal slowness of the heartbeat.
Brain
Mass of nerve tissue which is contained within the skull.
Bronchiectasis
Dilation of the narrowest portions of the breathing tubes of the lung.
Bronchitis
Inflammation of mucus membrane of bronchial tubes.
Buerger's Disease
Thromboangiitis obliterans; obliteration and inflammation of the larger arteries and veins of a limb by clotting and inflammation, involving nerve trunks.
Bursa
A lubricating sac usually found at pressure points or around joints.
Bursitis
Inflammation of the bursa.

C

Calcaneum
The os calcis, or heel bone.
Calcification
X-ray opaque substance found in serious tissues of the body.
Canthus
Either extremity of the slit between the eyelids.
Capitellum
Portion of bone found at the end of the arm bone.
Capsule
Fibrous membrane which envelopes an organ, joint or a foreign body.
Carbuncle
Group of boils resulting in localized gangrene or death of affected tissues.
Cardiac
Pertaining to the heart.
Cardiologist
Heart specialist.
Catheter
Hollow cylinder of silver, India rubber or other material, designed to be passed into a hollow area for drainage purposes.
Cartilage
White substance which covers ends of bones.
Causalgia
A painful condition.

Cellulitis

Diffuse inflammation of cellular tissue, i.e., especially loose cellular tissue just underneath skin.

Cephalalgia

Headache.

Cerebellum

Back part of the brain, concerned in coordination of movements.

Cerebrum

Front part of the brain, concerned with the conscious processes of the mind.

Cervix

Neck or neck-like part.

Charcot's joint

Painless joint destruction.

Cholecystectomy

Surgical removal of the gall-bladder.

Cholecystis

Inflammation of gall-bladder.

Cholelithiasis

Gallstone.

Chorio-Retinal

Relating to the visual tissue of eye and its supporting structure.

Chondral

Pertaining to cartilage.

Cicatrix

Scar.

Cirrhosis

Fibrosis or sclerosis of any organ; hardening.

Clavicle

Collar bone.

Clonus

Muscular spasm in which contraction and relaxation of muscle follow one another in rapid succession.

Coccydynia

Pain in the coccyx.

Coccygectomy

Removal of the coccyx.

Coccygeal

Relating to the coccyx.

Coccyx

Small bone at the end of the spinal column in man.

Congenital

Existing at birth.

Congestion

Engorgement of blood vessels of a part.

Conjunctiva

Delicate membrane which lines the inner surface of the eyelids and covers the eyeball in front.

Colles Fracture

Fracture of lower end of radius

Colon

The last part of the intestinal tract.

Comminuted
  Broken into more than two fragments.
Concussion
  Injury of a soft structure, as the brain, resulting from a blow or violent shaking.
Coronary Artery
  The artery providing nutrition to the heart muscle.
Cornea
  Transparent structure forming the anterior part of the external layer of eyeball.
Cortex
  Outer portion of an organ, such as the kidney, as distinguished from inner or medullary portion; external layer of gray matter covering hemispheres of cerebrum and cerebellum.
Costal
  Pertaining to the ribs.
Coxa
  Hip joint.
Cranium
  Skull.
Crepitus
  Abnormal sounds heard in the case of fractured bones and diseased tissues when rubbing together.
Curettage
  Scraping the interior of a cavity for the removal of tissue.
Cutaneous
  Relating to the skin.
Cyanosis
  Blueish discoloration of external tissue, e.g. lips, nails, skin.
Cyst
  Abnormal sac which contains a liquid or semi-solid.
Cystoscopy
  Inspection of the interior of the bladder with a cystoscope.
Cystostomy
  Formation of a more or less permanent opening into the urinary bladder.

D

Dactyl
  Digit: Finger or toe.
Decompensation
  Failure to maintain normal function as in heart failure.
Deltoid
  Triangular-shaped muscle of the shoulder.
Dementia
  Form of insanity.
Dermatitis
  Inflammation of the skin.
Dermatologist
  Skin specialist.
Dermaphytosis
  Skin disease due to presence of a vegetable microparasite.

Desiccation
The removal of tissue by chemical, physical, electrical, freezing, or x-ray.

Diabetes (Melitus)
A disease having symptoms of excessive urine and sugar excretion.

Diaphragm
Muscular partition between thorax and abdomen.

Diarrhea
Abnormally frequent discharge of fluid fecal matter from the bowel.

Diastasis
Simple separation of normally joined parts.

Diastole
Period of rest during which heart is filling up for next beat.

Diathermy
Local elevation of temperature in tissues, produced by special form of high-frequency current.

Diathesis
Predisposition to a disease.

Digit
Finger or toe.

Dilatation
Enlargement, due to stretching or thinning out of tissues.

Diplopia
Double-vision.

Disc
A round flat surface variously found in eye and spinal column conditions.

Dislocation
Most frequently used in orthopedics to describe a disturbance of normal relationship of bones which enter into formation of a joint.

Distal
Farthest from the point of origin; the term is usually used in connection with the extremities.

Diverticulum
Pouch or sac opening out from a tubular organ.

Dorsal
Relating to the back; posterior.

Dorsum
The back; upper or posterior surface or back of any part.

Duct
Tube or passage with well-defined walls for passing excretions or secretions.

Duodenum
Upper portion of intestinal tube connecting with stomach.

Dupuytren's Contraction
Contraction of the palmar fascia causing permanent flexion of one or more fingers.

Dura Mater
Outermost and toughest of three membranes covering brain and spinal cord.

Dysphagia
Difficulty in swallowing.

Dyspnoea
Difficulty in breathing.

Dysuria
Difficulty or pain in urination.

E

Ecchymosis
Black and blue spot on the skin.
Ectropion
A rolling outward of the margin of an eyelid.
Eczema
A form of dermatitis.
Edema
Swelling due to watery effusion in the intercellular spaces.
Electrocardiogram
Graph of electric currents in the heart.
Electrocardiograph
Instrument for producing electrocardiogram.
Embolus
Clot or plug brought by blood-current from distant part.
Embolism
The plugging up of a blood vessel by a floating mass.
Eminence
Circumscribed area raised above general area of surrounding surface.
Emphysema
Abnormal distention with loss of elasticity of the air sacs of the lung.
Empyema
Accumulation of pus or matter in normally closed cavity on the surface of the lung.
Encephalitis
Inflammation of the brain substance.
Encephalogram
Roentgenogram of contents of the skull.
Encephalopathy
Conditions of disease of the brain.
Endocrine Gland
A gland which furnishes internal secretion.
Endogenous
Originating or produced within organism or one of its parts.
Enophthalmos
Recession of the eyeball within the orbit.
Epicardium
Cover of the heart.
Epicondyle
Projection from long bone near articular extremity above or upon condyle.
Epidermis
Outermost layer of the skin.
Epididymis
Oblong or boat-shaped body located on back of testicle.
Epidural
Upon the outer envelope of the brain.
Epigastric
Depression at pit of abdominal wall at tip of sword-shaped cartilage of sternum.

Epilepsy, Jacksonian
Convulsive contractions affecting localized groups of muscles without disturbance of mentality.

Epiphysis
Ends of long bones.

Epistaxis
Bloody nose.

Epithelium
Covering of skin and mucus membrane consisting of epithelial cells.

Epithelioma
Cancer of the skin or mucus membrane.

Erector spinae
Muscle keeping the spine erects.

Eruption
A breaking out; redness, spotting or other visible phenomena on the skin or mucus membrane.

Erythema
Abnormal redness of the skin.

Esophagus
Gullet. Tube connecting mouth to stomach.

Etiology
Cause.

Eversion
A turning outward, as of the eyelid or foot.

Exacerbation
Increase in severity of disease or symptoms.

Excision
Operative removal of a portion of an organ.

Excrescence
Outgrowth from the surface, especially a pathological growth.

Exogenous
Originating or produced outside.

Exophthalmus
Protrusion or prominence of the eyeball.

Exostosis
Bony tumor springing from surface of a bone, most commonly seen at muscular attachments.

Extensor
A muscle the contraction of which tends to straighten a limb.

Extrasystole
Premature contraction of one or more heart chambers.

Exudate
A fluid, often coagulable, extravasated into tissue or cavity.

F

Facies
Face, countenance, expression; surface.

Fascia
Sheet or band of fibrous tissue.

Felon
Abscess in terminal phalanx of a finger.
Femoral
Relating to the femur or thigh.
Femur
Thigh bone.
Fibrillation
Totally irregular beat.
Fibroma
Fibroid tumor.
Fibrosis
Pathological formation of fibrous tissue.
Fibula
Smaller calf bone.
Fistula
Abnormal passageway leading to surface of body.
Flexion
Bending of a joint.
Flexor
A muscle the action of which is to flex a joint.
Follicle
Very small excretory or secretory sac or gland.
Foramen
Aperture through a bone or membranous structure.
Fracture, Comminuted
Bone broken into more than two pieces.
Fracture, Ununited
One in which union fails to occur.
Frontal
Relating to the front of body.
Fundus
Base of a hollow organ.
Fusiform
Spindle-shaped, tapering at both ends.

G

Ganglion
Usually used to describe a cystic tumor occurring on a tendon sheath or in connection with a joint.
Gangrene
Death or masse of any part of the body.
Gastric
Pertaining to the stomach.
Gastrocnemius
One of the calf muscles.
Genitalia
Organs of reproduction.
Genito-Urinary
Relation to reproduction and urination, noting organs concerned.

Genu

Knee

Genu-Valgum

Knock-knee.

Gladiolus

Middle and largest division of sternum (chest bone).

Gland

Secreting organ.

Glaucoma

Increased pressure in the eyeball.

Gluteal

Pertaining to the buttocks.

Greenstick Fracture

Incomplete fracture.

Gynecologist

Specialist in the treatment of diseases peculiar to women.

H

Hallux

Great toe.

Hallux valgus

Deviation of great toe toward inner or lateral side of the foot (bunion).

Haematemesis

Vomiting of blood.

Haemoglobin

Coloring matter of blood in red blood corpuscles.

Haemoptysis

Discharge of blood from the lungs by coughing.

Hemarthrosis

Effusion of blood into cavity of a joint.

Hematoma

Swelling formed by effused blood.

Hematuria

Passage of blood in the urine.

Hemianopsia

Loss of vision for one-half of visual field.

Hemorrhage

Bleeding, especially if profuse.

Hemorrhoids

Piles, a varicose condition causing painful swellings of the anus.

Hepatic

Pertaining to the liver.

Herania

Protrusion of organ outside of its normal confines.

Hernioplasty

Operation for hernia.

Herniotomy

Operation for relief of hernia.

Humerus
> Bone of the upper arm.

Hydrarthrosis
> Effusion of a serous fluid into a joint cavity.

Hydrocele
> Circumscribed collection of fluid around the testicle.

Hydrone Phrosis
> Dilatation inside kidney due to obstruction of flow of urine.

Hyperaesthesia
> Excessive sensitiveness of the skin to touch or hypersensitiveness of any special sense.

Hyperglycaemia
> Abnormally large proportion of sugar in blood.

Hypertension
> High blood pressure often associated with arteriosclerosis.

Hyperthrophy
> Enlargement, general increase in bulk of a part or organ, not due to tumor formation.

Hypogastrium
> Lower middle region of the abdomen.

Hypoplasia
> Under-development of structure.

Hypothenar
> Fleshy mass at the inner (little finger) side of the palm.

Hysteria
> A functional nervous condition characterized by lack of emotional control and sudden temporary attacks of mental, emotional or physical aberration.

I

Ileum
> Portion of the small intestine.

Ilium
> One of the bones of the pelvis.

Impacted
> Driven in firmly.

Incontinence
> Inability to retain a natural discharge.

Induration
> Hardening; spot or area of hardened tissue

Infarct
> Death of tissue due to lack of blood supply

Inguinal
> Relating to the groin.

In situ
> In position.

Intercostal
> Between the ribs

Interstitial
> Relating to spaces within any structure.

Intertrochanteric
> Between the two trochanters of the femur or thigh bone

Intervertebral
> Between two vertebrae.

Iris
> Circular colored portion of the eye which surrounds pupil

Ischaemia
> Local and temporary deficiency of blood.

Ischium
> One of the pelvic bones.

J

Jaundice
> Yellowness of tissues due to absorption of bile.

Jejunum
> Portion of small intestine about 8 feet long, between duodenum and ileum.

K

Kienboeck Disease
> Increased porosity and softness of certain carpal bones.

Keloid
> Peculiar overgrowth of hyaline connective tissues in the skin of predisposed individuals after injury or scarring.

Keratitis
> Inflammation of the cornea.

Kyphosis
> Curvature of the spine, hump-back, hunch-back.

L

Laceration
> Separation of tissue (cut).

Lacriminal
> Relating to the tears apparatus.

Laminae
> Flattened portions of the sides of a vertebral arch.

Laminectomy
> Removal of one or more laminae from the vertebrae.

Larynx
> Organ of voice production.

Lesion
> Any hurt, wound or degeneration.

Leucocytosis
> Temporary increase in relative number of white blood cells in the blood.

Leucopenia
> Abnormal decrease in number of white blood corpuscles.

Ligament
> Tough fibrous band which connects one bone with another.

Lipoma
> Tumor composed of fatty tissue.

Lordosis
> Anteroposterior curvature of the spine (opposite to kyphosis).

Lue tic
> Syphilitic.

Lumbar
> Lower back.

Lumbar Vertebrae
> The five vertebrae between the thoracic vertebrae and the sacrum.

Luxation
> Dislocation.

Lymphangitis
> Inflammation of the lymphatic vessels.

M

Malar
> Relating to the cheek-bone.

Malignant
> Resistant to treatment; occurring in severe form; tending to grow worse and (in the case of a tumor) to recur after removal. Usually indicates poor end result.

Malleoli
> Rounded bony prominences on both sides of the ankle joint.

Mandible
> Lower jaw.

Manubrium
> Upper portion of the sternum.

Mastectomy
> Amputation of the breast.

Maxilla
> Upper jaw.

Meatus
> Passage or opening.

Meninges
> Membranes, specifically the envelope of brain and spinal cord.

Meningitis
> Inflammation of the meninges.

Meniscus
> Intraarticular fibrocartilage of crescentic or discoid shape found in certain joints.

Mesentery
> Web or membrane connecting bowel tube to posterior abdominal wall (a portion of the peritoneum).

Metabolism
> The total operation of building up and breaking down tissues.

Metacarpus

Part of hand between wrist and fingers; palm; five metacarpal bones collectively which form skeleton of this part.

Metastasis

Transfer of disease, usually malignant, to remote part of the body.

Metatarsalgia

Pain in the region of the metatarsus(or ball of foot).

Metatarsus

Anterior portion of foot between instep and toes, having as its skeleton five long bones articulating anteriorly with the phalanges.

Mottling

Spotting with patches of varying shades of colors.

Mucocutaneous

Relating to mucus membrane and skin, noting the line of junction of the two at the nasal, oral, vaginal and anal orifices.

Musculature

Arrangement of muscles in a part or in the body as a whole.

Myalgia

Muscular pain.

Myelitis

Inflammation of the substance of the spinal cord.

Myelograph

X-ray picture of spinal cord using radio-opaque substance.

Myocardium

Heart Muscle.

Myocarditis

Inflammation of the muscular walls of the heart.

Myositis

Inflammation of a muscle.

N

Navicular

Boat-shaped, noting a bone in the wrist and one in the ankle.

Nausea

Sickness at the stomach; inclination to vomit.

Nephritis

Inflammation of the kidney.

Necrosis

Death en masse of a portion of tissue.

Nephrosis

Non-inflammatory disease of the kidney.

Neuralgia

Pain radiating along a nerve.

Neuritis

Inflammation of a nerve.

Neurologist

Nerve specialist.

Neuroma

Tumor made up largely of nerve tissue.

Neuropsychiatric
    Relating to disease of both mind and nervous system.
Neurosis
    Functional derangement of the nervous system.
Nocturia
    Bed-wetting.
Node
    Knob; circumscribed swelling; circumscribed mass of differentiated tissue; knuckle.
Nucleus Pulposus
    Gelatinous center of an intervertebral disc.
Nystagmus
    Continuous movement of the eyeballs in the horizontal or vertical plains.

O

Occipital
    Relating to the back of the head.
Occlude
    To close up or fit together.
Occular
    Relating to the eye; visual.
Occult
    Hidden; concealed, noting a concealed hemorrhage, the blood being so changed as not to be readily recognized.
Olecranon
    Tip of the elbow.
Omentum
    Web or apron-like membranous structure lying in front of the intestines.
Opacities
    Areas lacking in transparency.
Opthalmia
    Disease of the eye.
Opthalmologist
    Specialist in eye diseases and refractive errors of the eye.
Optic
    Relating to the eye or to vision.
Optometrist
    Person without medical training who fits glasses to correct visual defects.
Orbit
    Eye- socket.
Orchitis
    Inflammation of the testicle.
Orchidectomy
    Castration; removal of one or both testicles.
Orthopedics
    Branch of surgery which has to do with treatment of diseases of joints and spine and correction of deformities.
Orthopnea
    Ability to breathe with comfort only when sitting erect or standing.

Os
> Bone

Oscalcis
> Heel-bone.

Ossification
> Formation of bone; change into bone.

Osteoma
> Bone tumor.

Osteomyelitis
> Inflammation of bone and bone marrow.

Osteoporosis
> Disease of bone marked by increased porosity and softness ("thinning" of bone).

Osteotomy
> Cutting a bone, usually by saw or chisel, for removal of a piece of dead bone, correction of knock-knee or other deformity, or for any purpose whatsoever.

Otologist
> Specialist in diseases of the ear.

P

Paget's Disease
> Usually refers to a bone disease.

Pancreas
> Abdominal digestive gland, extending from duodenum to spleen, containing insulin forming cells.

Palate
> Roof of the mouth.

Palliative
> Mitigating; reducing in severity, noting a method of treating a disease or its symptoms.

Palmar
> Referring to the palm of the hand.

Palpate
> To examine by feeling and pressing with the palms and fingers.

Palpebral
> Relating to an, eyelid or the eyelids.

Papule
> Pimple.

Palsy
> Paralysis.

Paraesthesia
> Abnormal spontaneous sensation, such as a burning, pricking, numbness.

Paralysis
> Loss of power of motion.

Paralysis Agitans
> Shaking paralysis, Parkinson's Disease.

Paraplegia
> Paralysis of legs and lower parts of the body.

Paravertebral
Alongside a vertebra or the spinal column.
Parenchymal
Relating to the specific tissue of a gland or organ.
Paresis
Incomplete paralysis.
Parietal
Pertaining to the walls.
Parkinson's Syndrome
Aggregate symptoms, including raised eyebrows and expressionless face, of paralysis agitans.
Paronychia
Inflammation of structures surrounding the nail or the bone itself of finger or toe.
Paralysis Agitans
Shaking paralysis, Parkinson's Disease.
Paraplegia
Paralysis of legs and lower parts of the body.

Paravertebral
Alongside a vertebra or the spinal column.
Parenchymal
Relating to the specific tissue of a gland or organ.
Paresis
Incomplete paralysis.
Parietal
Pertaining to the walls.
Parkinson's Syndrome
Aggregate symptoms, including raised eyebrows and expressionless face, of paralysis agitans.
Paronychia
Inflammation of structures surrounding the nail or the bone itself of finger or toe.

Passive
Not active.
Past-Pointing
Test of integrity of vestibular apparatus of the ear by rotating person in revolving chair.
Patella
Knee-cap.
Pathology
Branch of medicine which treats of the abnormal tissues in disease.
Pectoral
Relating to the chest.
Pedicle
Stalk or stem forming the attachment of a tumor which is non-sessile, i.e., which does not have a broad base of attachment.
Pellegrini, Stieda's Disease
Bony growth over the internal condyle of the femur, a sequel of stieda's fracture.
Pendulous
Hanging freely or loosely.
Pericardium
Sac enveloping the heart.
Periosteum
Thick, fibrous membrane covering the entire surface of a bone.

Periphery
Outer part or surface.

Peristalsis
Worm-like movement of the gastro-intestinal tract.

Peritoneum
Serous membrane which covers abdominal organs and inner aspect of abdominal walls.

Peritonitis
Inflammation of the peritoneum.

Peroneal
Pertaining to the outer aspects of the leg.

Pes
Foot; foot-like or basal structure or part.

Pes Cavus
Exaggeration of the normal arch of the foot; hollowfoot.

Pes Equinus
Permanent extension of the foot so that only the ball rests on the ground.

Petechial
Relating to minute hemorrhagic spots, of pinpoint to pinhead size, in the skin.

Phalanx
Bone of a finger or toe.

Phlebitis
Inflammation of the veins.

Physiology
Science which treats of functions of different parts of the body.

Physiotherapy
Use of natural forces in the treatment of disease, as in electro-hydro, and aero-therapy, massage, and therapeutic exercises, and use of mechanical devices in mechanotherapy.

Pill-RollingTremor
Tremor in paralysis agitans in the form of circular movement of opposed tips of thumb and index finger.

Pilonidal Cyst
Cyst at the lower end of the spine.

Pisiform
Pea-shaped or pea-sized.

Plantar
Relating to the sole of the foot.

Pleura
Serous membrane which invests lungs and covers inner part of the chest walls (similar to peritoneum in abdominal cavity.)

Pleurisy
Inflammation of the pleura.

Plexus
Network or tangle of nerves.

Plumbism
Lead poisoning.

Pneumoconiosis
Dust disease of the lungs.

Pneumonia
Inflammation of lung substance.

Pneumonoconiosis
Fibrous hardening of the lungs due to irritation caused by inhalation of dust incident to various occupations.

Pneumothorax
Presence of air or gas in the pleural cavity.

Poliomyelitis
Inflammation of the anterior portion of the spinal cord.

Polyp
Pedunculated swelling or outgrowth from a mucus membrane.

Polyuria
Excessive excretion of urine.

Popliteal
Relating to the posterior surface of the knee.

Precordium
Anterior surface of lower part of the thorax.

Pretibial
Relating to anterior portion of the leg.

Proliferative
Excess growth.

Pronate
To rotate the forearm in such a way that the palm of the hand looks backward when the arm is in the anatomical position, or downward when the arm is extended at a right angle with the body.

Prostate
Gland surrounding neck of the male bladder.

Prostatectomy
Removal of all or part of the prostate.

Protuberance
Outgrowth: swelling; knob.

Proximal
Nearest the trunk or point of origin, said of part of an extremity, artery or nerve so situated.

Psychiatrist
Alienist; one who specializes in diseases of the mind.

Psychogenic
Of mental origin or causation.

Ptosis
Drooping down of an eyelid or an organ.

Pubic
One of the bones of the pelvis.

Pulmonic
Relating to the lungs.

Puritis
Itching irritation.

Purulent
Having the appearance of pus or matter.

Pyelitis
Inflammation of a portion of the kidney.

Pyelogram
Roentgenogram of the area of the kidneys and ureter, by use of opaque substances.

Pyogenic
> Pus-forming.

R

Radiologist
> One skilled in the diagnostic and therapeutic use of x-rays.

Radius
> Outer and shorter of the two bones of forearm.

Rales
> Sounds of varied character heard on auscultation of the chest in cases of disease of the lungs or bronchi.

Rectum
> Terminal portion of the digestive tube.

Reflex
> Involuntary or reflected action or movement.

Renal
> Pertaining to the kidney.

Resection
> Removal of articular ends of one or both bones forming a joint, or of a segment of any part, such as the intestine.

Respiration
> Function common to all living plants or animals, consisting in taking in of oxygen and throwing off products of oxidation in the tissues, mainly carbon dioxide and water.

Retina
> Inner, nervous tunic of the eyeball, consisting of an outer pigment layer and an inner layer formed by expansion of the optic nerve.

Retrosternal
> Behind the sternum.

Rib
> One of twenty-four elongated curved bones forming the main portion of bony wall of the chest.

Rhinitis
> Inflammation of the nasal mucus membrane.

Roentgenologist
> One skilled in the diagnostic and therapeutic use of x-rays.

S

Sacroiliac
> Relating to sacrum and ilium, noting articulation between the two bones and associated ligaments.

Sacrum
> Triangular bone at the base of the spine.

Sarcoma
> Malignant tumor of fibrous tissue or its derivatives.

Scaphoid
> Boat-shaped; hollowed.

Scapula

Shoulder-blade.

Sciatica

Painful affection of the sciatic nerve.

Sclerosis

Hardness

Scoliosis

Lateral curvature of the spine.

Scrotum

Sac containing testes.

Semilunar Cartilages

Two intraarticular fibrocartilages of the knee-joint.

Senile

Relating to or characteristic of old age.

Septicemia

Morbid condition due to presence of septic microbes and their poisons in the blood.

Sequela

Morbid condition following as a consequence of another disease.

Sesamoid.

Resembling in size or shape a grain of sesame.

Sequestrum

Piece of dead bone separated from living bone.

Shock

Sudden vital depression due to injury or emotion which makes an untoward depression.

Siderosis

Form of dust disease due to presence of iron dust.

Silicosis

Form of dust disease due to inhalation of stone dust.

Sinusitis

Inflammation of the lining membrane of any sinus, especially of one of the accessory sinuses of the nose.

Spasm

Sudden violent involuntary rigid contraction, due to muscular action.

Sphincter

Orbicular muscle which, when in state of normal contraction, closes one of the orifices of the body.

Spina Bifida

Limited defect in the spinal column consisting in absence of vertebral arches, through which defect spinal membranes protrude.

Spondylolisthesis

Forward subluxation of body of vertebra on vertebra below it or on sacrum.

Sprain

Wrenching of a joint.

Stenosis

Narrowing of an orifice.

Sternoclavicular

Relating to sternum and clavicle, noting an articulation and occasional muscle.

Stricture

Abnormal narrowing of a channel.

Supinate

To turn forearm and hand volar side uppermost.

Suture

Stitch.

Symphysis

Union between two bones by means of fibrocartilage.

Syncope

Fainting.

Syndrome

Complex of symptoms which occur together.

Synovitis

Inflammation of synovial membrane, especially of a joint.

Systole

Period of the heart-beat during which the heart is contracting.

T

Tachycardia

Abnormal increase in rate of the hearts beat, not subsiding on rest, sudden in onset and offset.

Tarsus

Root of the foot or instep.

Temporamandibular

Relating to the temporal bone (bone of the temple) and lower jaw, noting the articulation of the lower jaw.

Tendon

Inelastic fibrous cord or band in which muscle fibers ends and by which muscle is attached to bone or other structure.

Tendosynovitis

Inflammation of the sheath of a tendon.

Tetanus

Lockjaw.

Thorax

Chest, upper part of the trunk between neck and abdomen; it is formed by the twelve dorsal vertebrae, the twelve pairs of ribs, sternum, and muscles and fascias attached to these; it is separated from the abdomen by the diaphragm; it contains chief organs of circulatory and respiratory systems.

Thrombo Angitis Obliterans

Buerger's disease; obliteration of the larger arteries and veins of a limb by thrombi, with subsequent gangrene. See Buerger's Disease.

Thrombophlebitis

Thrombosis with inflammation of the veins.

Thrombosis

Formation of a clot of blood within a blood vessel.

Thyroid

Gland and cartilage of the larynx.

Thyroidectomy

Removal of the thyroid gland.

Tibia

Shin-bone; inner and larger of two bones of the leg.

Tinnitus

Subjective noises (ringing, whistling, booming, etc.) in the ears.

Tonsillitis

Inflammation of a tonsil.

Torticollis

Wry-neck; stiff-neck; spasmodic contraction of muscles of the neck; the head is drawn to one side and usually rotated so that the chin points the other side.

Torsion

Twisting or rotation of a part upon its axis; twisting the cut end of an artery to arrest hemmorhage.

Toxemia

Blood-poisoning.

Toxin

Poison.

Trachea

Windpipe.

Transillumination

Shining light through a translucent part to see if fluid is present.

Trapezius

Muscle extending from back of the head to shoulderbiade; it moves head and shoulder.

Trauma

Wound; injury inflicted usually more or less suddenly by physical agent.

Tremor

Trembling, shaking, loss of equilibrium.

Trephine

Cylindrical or crown saw used for removal of a disc of bone, especially from the skull, or of other firm tissue as that of the cornea.

Triceps

Three-headed muscle extending the forearm. (Covers posterior of upper arm).

Trochanter

One of two bony prominences developed from independent osseous centers near the upper extremity of the thigh bone.

Tubercle

Circumscribed, rounded, solid elevation on the skin, mucus membrane, or surface of an organ; lesion of tuberculosis consisting of a small isolated nodule or aggregation of nodules.

Tuberosity

Broad eminence of bone.

U

Ulcer

Open sore other than a wound.

Ulna

Inner and larger of the two bones of the forearm.

Umbilicus

Navel.

Ununited

Not united or knit, noting an unhealed fracture.

Ureter
Musculomembranous tube leading from kidney to bladder.

Urethra
Membranous tube leading from bladder to external exit.

Urination
The passing of urine.

Urogram
Roentgenogram of any part (kidneys, ureters, bladder) of the urinary tract, with the use of opaque substances.

Urologist
One versed in the branch of medical science which has to do with urine and its modifications in disease.

Urtcaria
Hives.

Uterus
Womb.

V

Varicocele
Varicose veins of the spermatic cord.

Varicose
Dilated, as used in reference to veins.

Varix
Enlarged and tortuous vein, artery, or lymphatic vessel.

Vas
Vessel.

Vasomotor
Regulating mechanism controlling expansion and contraction of blood vessels.

Ventral
Relating to anterior portion.

Ventricular
Relating to a ventricle.

Vertebra
One of thirty-three bones of the spinal column.

Vertex
Crown of the head; topmost point of the vault of the skull.

Vertigo
Dizziness.

Vitiligo
Appearance on the skin of white patches of greater or lesser extent, due to simple loss of pigment without other trophic changes.

Volar
Referring to the palm of the hand.

Z

Zygoma
Strong bar of bone bridging over the depression of the temple; cheek-bone.

CPSIA information can be obtained
at www.ICGtesting.com
Printed in the USA
LVHW061609240720
661452LV00010B/379